Muscle Car BRAKE UPGRADES

HOW TO DESIGN, SELECT, AND INSTALL

Bobby Kimbrough

S-A DESIGN

CarTech®

CarTech®

CarTech®, Inc.
838 Lake Street South
Forest Lake, MN 55025
Phone: 651-277-1200 or 800-551-4754
Fax: 651-277-1203
www.cartechbooks.com

Edit by Bob Wilson
Layout by Hailey Samples

ISBN 978-1-61325-271-0
Item No. SA371

Library of Congress Cataloging-in-Publication Data
Names: Kimbrough, Bobby, 1961- author.
Title: Muscle car brake upgrades : how to design, select, and install /
Bobby Kimbrough.
Description: Forest Lake, MN : CarTech, [2019]
Identifiers: LCCN 2019006296 | ISBN 9781613252710
Subjects: LCSH: Automobiles–Brakes.
Classification: LCC TL269 .K5355 2019 | DDC 629.2/460288–dc23
LC record available at https://lccn.loc.gov/2019006296

Written, edited, and designed in the U.S.A.
Printed in China
10 9 8 7 6 5 4 3 2 1

CarTech books may be purchased at a discounted rate in bulk
for resale, events, corporate gifts, or educational purposes. Special editions may also be created to specification. For details,
contact Special Sales at 838 Lake Street S., Forest Lake, MN
55025 or by email at sales@cartechbooks.com.

DISTRIBUTION BY:

Europe
PGUK
63 Hatton Garden
London EC1N 8LE, England
Phone: 020 7061 1980 • Fax: 020 7242 3725
www.pguk.co.uk

Australia
Renniks Publications Ltd.
3/37-39 Green Street
Banksmeadow, NSW 2109, Australia
Phone: 2 9695 7055 • Fax: 2 9695 7355
www.renniks.com

Canada
Login Canada
300 Saulteaux Crescent
Winnipeg, MB, R3J 3T2 Canada
Phone: 800 665 1148 • Fax: 800 665 0103
www.lb.ca

CONTENTS

DEDICATION

To my wife, Marcy, whose love and support made this entire effort possible. To my sons, Andrew and Kelly, my daughter-in-law, Hannah, my grandsons, Cayden and Harrison, and granddaughter, Aureli, I appreciate all the time you gave up so that I could pursue the completion of this book. It wasn't easy to be missing a family member all those days and weekends. Last, but certainly not least, to my loyal companion, Turbo the Wonderdog. Nobody does a project like this alone. Your combined support during those long days and nights made all the difference. This book, and everything within its pages, is dedicated to all of you.

ACKNOWLEDGMENTS

My life has centered around maintenance from the time I was born. I performed my first brake job in the 1970s, and I have changed every brake pad and rotor on my personal vehicles since that time. Sometimes it was out of financial necessity (I couldn't afford to pay someone else to do it) and sometimes out of desire. Even with extensive experience over a range of domestic and foreign cars, there is always more to learn. It takes a village, and in my case a fairly large town, to raise a proficient brake technician. I wish to acknowledge some of the people who contributed to this project.

Without car enthusiasts, none of this is needed or practical. Everything we do in the automotive aftermarket revolves around the end user: the car nut. Acknowledgements would not be complete without a tip of the hat to all the muscle car fanatics. Thank you.

One of the many people who helped with this book is Mr. Ed Zinke. He put me in contact with the right people to get answers and is also a valued personal friend. Ed is a highly respected media professional who was awarded SEMA's Robert E. Petersen Media Person of the Year award. His insight and contacts were invaluable when I needed very specific help.

Todd Ryden's unwavering support and help ensured this project got off the ground from the beginning. His photography support and knowledge about the different brake systems filled in the gaps in my own experience. His words were the glue that bound the rest of the work together. I have enjoyed our collaborations and can't wait for the next one to occur.

Longtime friend and brake systems expert Michael Hamrick provided much of the information from Wilwood Engineering. For a full year he was willing to take my calls and answer my emails full of questions, expecting nothing in return. Much of the work within this book was possible because of his help.

Cathy White of Classic Performance Products (CPP) assisted with specialized material and information on OEM replacement brake systems. Cathy pulled back the curtains and showed the inner workings of CPP's manufacturing process. That information was critical in the composition of this book.

My "go-to" guy on brakes has always been Mark Chichester of Master Power Brakes. His honesty and integrity put him at the top of my list. He is very quotable, as evidenced by the many Chichester quotes within these pages.

Todd Gartshore was a force in the industry and the face of Baer Brakes for many years. Todd helped me and many new writers understand how media and brake systems work. When Todd passed away, there was a massive hole that needed to be filled. Rick Elam has stepped up and filled that void. I will always cherish what Todd and Rick have done to support the industry.

Adam Keiser at Performance Friction Brakes helped connect the points for high-performance brake systems. His support was added late in the progress of this work, making me regret not reaching out to him sooner. The next time I attempt a brake project like this, he will be my first contact.

Jeff Smith, one of the most experienced technical writers on the planet and personal inspiration, played a huge role in this book. His invisible hand guided much of the work done here. My friend and employer, James Lawrence, served as my role model in digging for information. I used his questioning technique to drill down to the core of a subject.

Many of my current and a few of my past coworkers at Power Automedia are responsible for moral and mental support during the arduous hours of compiling information and organizing it into a workable form. Scott Parker, Andrew Almazon, Brittany Poleon, Kaley Lione, Michael Harding, April Taylor, Lloyd Hunt, Kevin McIntosh, and David Cruikshank are all responsible for providing the motivation to keep going. Shawn Brereton's push to keep an eye on quality reporting put an edge on the total project. It is a pleasure to know and work with people of this caliber.

My personal friends and industry leaders, Jason Snyder and Brian Shephard, helped keep my focus on the task at hand. Brian led by doing; Jason led with firm guidance. Special thanks to Kevin Shaw for reminding me why these documents are so important. It is hard work, but worth it in the long run.

For every gearhead, the people that always seem to go unrecognized are the neighbors who are subjected to a rusty junkyard of project cars and beating and banging at all hours of the day and night. I'm fortunate to have the most understanding neighbors and recognize the tolerance of Dave and Pattie Nellis. Dave is always there to hold a flashlight, fetch a wrench, or push a broken car. I may have been able to do this book without you, but I would not have wanted to.

Finally, my personal mentor and teacher, Ed Justice Jr., inspired the will and desire to do something that may help other enthusiasts. Ed and his family have always gone the extra mile to preserve automotive history and help forge new technology in the automotive aftermarket industry. The Justice family talks the talk by walking that straight line every day. Without Ed's leading by example and his sage guidance, I would have never attempted anything of this magnitude.

Anyone who has taken on the task or authoring a book knows the mountain of work involved. Without this village of support, no publication would ever get done.

INTRODUCTION

The aftermarket automotive brake industry has responded to vintage muscle car needs with modern technology that rivals anything produced by the automakers these days.

Henry Kissinger was famously quoted in the *New York Times* (January 19, 1971) as having said, "Power is the great aphrodisiac." He could very well have been talking about the muscle car era when he said that because muscle cars were built around power and sex appeal during the 1960s and early 1970s. It's easy to look back and see that American muscle cars produced during that period were the beginnings of what became known as supercars.

Arguably, the muscle car era started when Oldsmobile took the 6-cylinder Olds 76 platform and shoved a powerful V-8 under the hood. Taking a lighter-weight chassis and body and then combining that with a potent engine, the Oldsmobile Rocket 88 provided the framework for American speed. Within a matter of years, the other car companies responded with their own muscle cars. Chrysler's impressive Hemi engine found a home in the 1955 Chrysler C-300 and was crowned as "America's Most Powerful Car." At the same time, General Motors released the mouse that roared with its small-block V-8. This lighter-weight engine platform, which would become the GM standard for the next 50 years, helped create the lightweight muscle cars that followed.

Automobiles continued to become faster globally. The European auto racing scene was especially growing in popularity with its powerful and lightweight purpose-built race cars. All was well and the auto racing sector was enjoying great acceptance with the public until a tragedy at the 1955 Le Mans race when Mercedes driver Pierre Levegh touched another car, careening into the stands at 150 mph. The car's fuel tank ruptured and the car exploded into flames, resulting in the deaths of 84 people, including Levegh. Known as the most catastrophic accident in motorsports history, this led to a ban on factory-sponsored auto racing as agreed upon by the Automobile Manufacturers Association (AMA) in 1957.

It was the president of General Motors, Harlow Curtice, who suggested the self-imposed ban to prevent government action against racing activities. This worked well and kept many of the world's governments from creating laws to cease dangerous automobile racing, but the Association's carmakers were struggling to keep up with carmakers that were not in the AMA and the ban was lifted in 1963.

By this time, the 1962 Dodge Dart was already raising eyebrows, as it turned 13-second quarter-mile times at the drag strip. The familiar combination of a powerful engine and lightweight chassis returned in 1963 with the Pontiac Super Duty and its infamous "Swiss cheese" frame that was riddled with lightening holes. Ford began developing powerful personal coupes and adding a monstrous engine in full-size cars. Pontiac's chief designer, John DeLorean, had correctly assessed that youthful car buyers were looking for power in their new cars, and the Pontiac crew secretly began offering a 389-ci engine in its 1964 Pontiac Tempest GTO as an option.

GM's Chevrolet crew rolled out the Chevelle at first with the 327-ci small-block to stay within the company's guidelines on engine size for its midsize cars. However, the design crew abandoned that directive in 1965 when the 396 was installed, breaking the doors to the muscle car era wide open. The battle was on, and once again, speeds went up as the power in these machines increased. Pushing the edge of the speed envelope, it seemed as if nothing could stop these muscle cars, including the factory brake systems.

The original equipment manufacturer (OEM) brakes worked well as long as every car on the highway was going 65 mph and every car was equipped with drum brakes. When front-wheel disc brakes started showing up as an option and lighter foreign cars with better brake systems could stop faster on the roads, drum brake cars were at a disadvantage and less safe. In 1968, the federal government's safety and emissions rules came into play. Among the safety issues addressed in these stan-

Aftermarket wheels have differing brake spacing requirements. Be sure to check with the wheel manufacturer before purchasing a disc brake upgrade kit.

dards were dual-cylinder hydraulic brake systems and front disc brakes. It was obvious that braking systems needed to catch up with the power and speed capabilities of these muscle cars.

Owning one of these classic muscle cars today is an investment and a matter of great pride, but they are technologically more unsafe than ever. Modern braking systems have applied science that was unthinkable 40 years ago. Antilock braking, fade-resistant brake pads, and an improved pedal feel from improved braided steel lines instead of rubber brake hoses are available in upgrade kits for vintage cars. Critical upgrades include antilock brakes with the ability to maintain steering control under panic-braking situations and kits that allow older-style drum brakes to be replaced with disc brakes for the front wheels, where most of the effective braking takes place as the weight balance transfers forward.

In this book, we will cover the theory and history of braking systems as they apply to muscle cars, discuss the parts and functions of those components, and show three different upgrades in a trio of

different muscle car platforms from the Big Three American car manufacturers. These muscle cars were chosen because they are representative of the manufacturers and other cars in their product line. GM's Chevrolet Chevelle is similar to GM muscle cars from the Nova all the way to the Olds 442. Chrysler's Dodge Dart fills in for the Plymouth Barracuda and Road Runner and the Dodge Polara, Satellite, Coronet, Challenger, Charger, and Super Bee. Finally, the Ford Fairlane captures the essence of the Galaxie, Torino, Talladega, and Mercury Cyclone. We conclude the book with a chapter that helps the enthusiast determine his or her needs and develop a plan to execute the build strategy.

While we have attempted to cover most of the common aspects that will be encountered with a brake system upgrade, attention should be paid to aftermarket wheels and trends with larger wheels. Larger discs require extra room, and many times the spacing on aftermarket wheels can make things difficult. Checking with the wheel manufacturer is critical when upgrading to larger aftermarket brake systems.

THE EVOLUTION OF MUSCLE CARS AND BRAKES

Vehicles are a collection of several systems; some are more glamorous or more complicated than others. An incredible amount of attention is paid to the engine, which includes the lubrication and cooling subsystems. The ignition system and the electrical system offer very complicated components and schemes. The all-important drivetrain can include iconic names, such as *rock-crusher, floater,* or *posi-traction.* Even the more basic systems, such as suspension, steering, and exhaust, have garnered more consideration by enthusiasts than brakes. Yet, braking systems have seen equally impressive technological gains in the past 50 years. Individual system scrutiny aside, no other genre of automobile has benefitted from improved braking more than American muscle cars.

While factory brakes have improved over the years, there is no one-size-fits-all solution. There is an entire aftermarket auto industry built up around automotive brakes. Each manufacturer has several different lines, all tailored to a specific purpose and application.

Muscle cars started to show more power in the early 1960s, but this 1963 Chevy Biscayne represented the last year that Chevrolet officially supported racing. In 1964, General Motors ceased involvement in racing along with Chrysler and Ford. That did not stop some of the designers from building cars for the street with some muscle that was not overly promoted in advertising. Acceleration was improving, but stopping was developing proportionately in some of the high-performance models.

American Motors Muscle Cars Front Disc Brake Offerings

AMC AMX 1968–1970: The "Go Package" option included front disc brakes starting in 1968.

AMC Javelin 1967–1974: The "Go Package" option included front disc brakes starting in 1968.

AMC Matador 1970–1975: The "Go Package" option included front disc brakes starting in 1970.

Rambler Rebel 1957–1960/1966–1967: Drum brakes were standard in all years. ■

A 1974 AMC Javelin is shown here. The AMC Javelin was manufactured and marketed by AMC across two different generations in the peak of the muscle car era: 1968–1970 and 1971–1974. The Javelin was popular in drag racing and SCCA Trans Am series. (Photo Courtesy Power AutoMedia)

A Brief History of Muscle Cars

Merriam-Webster defines a muscle car as "any of a group of American-made two-door sports cars with powerful engines designed for high-performance driving." For our purposes, a muscle car is an American-made, two-door midsize or full-size car with a V-8 engine that is built for four or more passengers, was originally designed for street use, and was sold at an affordable price for younger buyers.

Almost every serious automotive historian considers the 1949 Oldsmobile Rocket 88 the first true muscle car. Using its new overhead valve V-8 in a lighter body that was designed for a 6-cylinder, Oldsmobile broke new ground in automotive design.

The fledgling NASCAR series was becoming the testing ground for midsize and full-size late-model cars. In the second year of the Grand National Series, the 1949/1950 Olds Rocket 88 won 10 times out of the 19 races held. A 1949 Lincoln won the first two races, a 1950 Mercury won

twice, a new Ford won once, and Plymouth won four races. It didn't take long for the car companies to realize that car sales for a model went up after winning an event. "Win on Sunday and sell on Monday" became the mantra. The new Oldsmobile even won the inaugural Carrera Panamericana.

Other manufacturers scrambled to duplicate Oldsmobile's success, using the same game plan: a powerful engine in a light body. Most carmakers brought out limited- and special-edition cars to demonstrate their capabilities on the track. Oldsmobile maintained its dominance in 1951 before giving way to the Hudson Hornet in 1952. It wasn't until 1955, when Chrysler brought out its C-300, that a true purpose-built muscle car hit the market. Chrysler was not shy about advertising its Hemi-powered family car as "America's Most Powerful Car."

Rambler, in an effort to battle with the Big Three, debuted its popular Rebel sedan. The Rebel was lightning quick for its time; when it

Vintage drum brake systems and reproduction drum brake systems are still very popular with hot rodders and street rodders. These groups seldom drive their vehicles and certainly don't risk their safety with modern highway speeds in crowded traffic.

was equipped with the optional Bendix electronic fuel injection (EFI), the Rebel sedan was recorded faster

General Motors Muscle Cars Front Disc Brake Offerings

Here is a 1970 Pontiac GTO 455. The Pontiac GTO was the third best-selling intermediate muscle car for the year and the era. There were only six GTOs ordered with the 1970-only D-Port 455 HO 360-hp package.

Buick Skylark 1961–1972: Power brakes were offered in 1953.

Chevrolet Camaro 1967–1975: Front disc brakes were optional starting in 1967. Front disc brakes were standard on SS models from 1968.

Chevrolet Chevelle 1964–1975: Front disc brakes were optional starting in 1967. Front disc brakes were standard in 1973.

Chevrolet Chevy II / Nova 1961–1975: Power brakes were offered in 1968. Front disc brakes were optional on the 1968 Nova SS and standard in 1969. All Novas had standard front disc brakes in 1975.

Chevrolet El Camino 1964–1975: Front disc brakes were optional starting in 1967 and standard in 1973.

Chevrolet Impala 1957–1975: Power brakes were offered in 1961. Optional front disc brakes started in 1969.

Chevrolet Malibu 1964–1975: Optional front disc brakes started in 1967.

Chevrolet Monte Carlo 1970–1975: Front disc brakes were standard from 1970.

Oldsmobile 88 1949–1975: Power brakes were offered in 1953. Front disc brakes were optional in 1967 and standard in 1971.

Oldsmobile 442 1964–1975: Optional front disc brakes started in 1967.

Oldsmobile Cutlass 1961–1975: Optional front disc brakes started in 1967 and were standard in 1973.

Oldsmobile Cutlass Supreme 1965–1975: Optional front disc brakes started in 1967 and were standard in 1973.

Pontiac Bonneville 1958–1972: Front disc brakes became standard in 1971.

Pontiac Grand Prix 1962–1972: Power brakes were offered in 1963. Optional front disc brakes started in 1967 and were standard in 1971.

Pontiac GTO 1964–1974: Optional front disc brakes started in 1967.

Pontiac LeMans 1964–1974: Optional front disc brakes started in 1967.

Pontiac Tempest 1961–1970: Optional front disc brakes started in 1967. ∎

from a standing start than the 1957 Chevrolet Corvette with its mechanical fuel injection. Up to the early 1960s, the powerful muscle cars from Detroit had not developed enough power that the conventional drum braking systems were overwhelmed yet. That was soon to change.

The Golden Era of Muscle Cars

As performance in automobiles grew, so did the popularity. While General Motors attempted to remain true to the racing ban, Dodge, Plymouth, Chrysler, and Ford began to battle it out on tracks across the land. However, things were about to change, as Chevrolet introduced the Super Sport (SS) option on the 1961 Impala. Along with the monstrous 409-ci engine, the package included tires, suspension, upgraded power brakes, and metallic brake linings.

The turning point came in 1964 when the GM floodgates opened. Buick, Chevrolet, Oldsmobile, and Pontiac entered their own purpose-built muscle cars, sliding them past GM's brass by labeling the upgrades as *heavy-duty* and not *high-performance*. The self-imposed

John DeLorean's Pontiac GTO was a game changer in the muscle car era. The original options on the GTO included metallic brake drum linings. Even DeLorean realized that more horsepower required better braking options.

ban was on racing, not street performance, so the new (and younger) designers and managers in the GM automotive divisions took advantage of street enthusiasts' passion and built cars for them. GM's standing rule of limiting economy and midsize cars to 330 ci was dramatically pushed beyond the line by John DeLorean, then president of the Pontiac division, with the Pontiac GTO.

The Pontiac GTO began as an option package for the Pontiac Tempest and was a project led directly by DeLorean. It was powered by Pontiac's 389-ci V-8 engine that was so successful in racing that it was dubbed the "Trophy V8." The package also included a floor-shifted 3-speed manual transmission with a Hurst shifter and linkage and optional tri-power carburetion. Among the many upgrades listed were metallic brake drum linings, showing that engineers were starting to take speed and traffic safety into consideration. Original production was limited to just 5,000 units.

The car was much more popular than even DeLorean expected, and General Motors was inspired to produce more cars for power-hungry street performance car devotees. Along with GM's confidence, other carmakers were prompted to imitate Pontiac's best seller. It was this keeping up with the Joneses mentality that slowed down the evolution of brakes in muscle cars during the 1960s. The public wanted more powerful cars at

Early Chevelle two-door coupes have been one of the most popular muscle cars to restore and modify, such as this 1965 Chevelle. Once enthusiasts add more muscle to these midsize muscle cars, disc brake upgrades should be seriously considered.

Ford Motor Company Muscle Cars Front Disc Brake Offerings

Ford Custom (500) 1964–1974: Front and rear drum brakes were offered, except the Custom 500 that had front disc brakes from 1972.

Ford Fairlane 1955–1970: Power disc brakes were an option starting in 1969.

Ford Fairlane Thunderbolt 1964: Front and rear drum brakes only were offered.

Ford Falcon 1960–1970: Power brakes were offered starting in 1964. Front and rear drum brakes only were offered.

Ford Galaxie 1958–1974: Power front disc brakes were optional in 1967 and standard starting in 1974.

Ford Mustang 1965–1973: The 1965 GT version was offered with front disc brakes. Optional power front disc brakes were offered for all models in 1967 and standard on the GT.

Ford Ranchero 1966–1975: Power front disc brakes were optional in 1968.

Ford Starliner 1960–1961: Front and rear drum brakes only were offered.

Ford Thunderbird 1955–1975: Power front disc brakes were optional in 1965.

Ford Torino 1968–1975: Front disc brakes and power assist were options in 1967. Power front disc brakes became standard on the Torino Squire Wagon in 1970 and all Torino models in 1972.

Mercury Comet 1960–1975: The GT package came with front disc brakes in 1966.

Mercury Cougar 1967–1975: Power front disc brakes were optional in some special models as early as 1969 but became standard in 1973.

Mercury Cyclone 1964–1971: The GT package came with front disc brakes in 1966. ∎

A 1963 Falcon Sprint is shown here. Ford general manager Robert S. McNamara commissioned a team to create a car that was small by American standards but would be considered midsize elsewhere in the world. The Falcon became a favorite budget car for hot rodders to soup up.

budget prices, and Detroit automakers gave it to them.

The Dodge Dart, Ford Fairlane, and Chevrolet Chevelle are great examples of muscle cars from the golden era of American muscle cars. Because they are a great representation of the genre, these cars were selected to represent each of the Big Three manufacturers with the upgrades shown in this book.

Drum Brakes

A crude form of mechanical drum brakes actually appeared on a Daimler creation in 1899. It was a simple design that was nothing more than a cable wrapped around a drum. The cable was anchored to the vehicle's chassis and controlled by the driver. Wilhelm Maybach improved upon the design on a Mercedes-Benz by using multiple steel cables wrapped around two drums on the rear wheels and controlled by a hand brake lever.

Despite these early efforts that encompassed the basic idea of drum brakes, Louis Renault is usually credited with the invention of drum brakes in 1902. Renault's form of drum brakes would become the standard for automobiles for the next 70 years.

In drum brakes, brake shoes generate friction by rubbing against the inner surface of a brake drum that is attached to a wheel. There are external-contracting brakes (in which the brake band surrounds the drum) and internal-expanding drum brakes (in which the shoes, supported by a back plate, are forced outward against the drum).

Modern automotive brakes can be broken down into two basic types: disc or drum. While it can be argued that removing your foot from the accelerator pedal can be a form of braking (deceleration), this book only includes systems that have hard components that are designed specifically for stopping.

Air brakes, which were originally developed for railway use, have been adopted for use on larger vehicles. Air brakes are usually a complicated system of reservoirs, valves, and a multi-circuit control system that make this type of braking too sophisticated for passenger car use. Current air brake systems must be operated differently than the more common hydraulic systems, and most countries require additional training and licensing to legally drive any vehicle using an air brake system. Neither magnetic brake or electrical brake systems are currently used in passenger cars.

Muscle cars from the golden era, such as this 1966 Chevelle, are prime candidates for brake and wheel upgrades to match modern performance. There are several aftermarket brake companies that support these muscle car brake upgrades. Baer Brakes, Classic Performance Products (CPP), Disc Brakes Australia (DBA) USA, Power Brake, Master Power Brakes, Stainless Steel Brakes Corporation (SSBC), TBM Brakes (formerly known as The Brake Man), and Wilwood are all representatives in the performance brake market.

Modern rotor designs include a scalloped version for serious racing applications. Scalloped rotors are specifically designed to reduce surface area, which effectively reduces weight. Saving weight in race applications is critical for obvious reasons. (Photo Courtesy Wilwood Engineering Inc.)

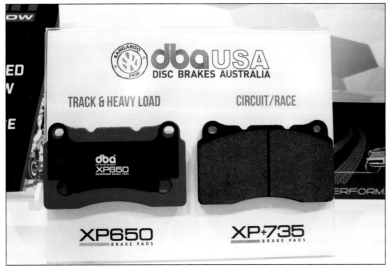

Disc Brakes Australia (DBA) USA is one of many modern companies that make brake pads with a variety of different materials. Brake pads are generally broken down into three groups: organic, ceramic, and semimetallic. However, each of these groups are made up of many different types of materials. For example, organic brake pads can be manufactured from various organic compounds, such as carbon, glass, rubber, or Kevlar. Semimetallic will be made with iron, steel, copper, or graphite in the friction material. Ceramics tend to be made of a manufacturer-specific ceramic compound. Each type has its own pros and cons.

Brake linings and the materials used have seen dramatic changes since their first application in 1888. Various soft metals have been used with noisy results. Asbestos linings worked well but posed a health hazard, so their use was stopped. Synthetic fibers have taken over the lead role in brake lining material. Use caution when dealing with older brake shoes like these. Avoid breathing the dust and try not to disturb the dust and fibers with compressed air or vacuum cleaners.

Disc Brakes and Brake Pad Linings

British inventor William Lanchester patented the disc brake in 1902, which was little more than soft copper brake pad linings that moved against a metal disc, transferring heat better but screeching brutally when applied.

Another British inventor, Herbert Frood, developed brake pads using asbestos as the lining. This quieted the braking action and gave Frood acknowledgment as the inventor of the brake pad by having developed a more efficient frictional surface. Asbestos was used in brake linings into the 1980s, when health concerns forced the mineral's removal from the automotive industry.

In the United States, one of the first to manufacture drum brakes was the A. H. Raymond Co. of Bridgeport, Connecticut, which opened in 1902 as a four-man shop that built brakes, brake linings, and clutch facings. Renamed Royal Equipment Co. by 1904, the company continued to improve brakes, particularly with a natural silica material called asbestos and copper-wire brake lining known as Raybestos.

These Raybestos brake linings were sold as double acting brakes. Advertising reported the double action as the ability to stop forward or backward motion. This claim left motorists believing that stopping in both directions was impossible before.

Duesenberg began putting brakes on the front wheels as well as the rear wheels in races during the 1915 events. This allowed the cars to carry speed longer before braking to enter corners. This setup required the driver to use a separate foot brake and hand brake to control the braking. A unit that combined both brakes into one pedal to operate the four brakes didn't come along until 1919.

Chrysler Corporation Muscle Cars Front Disc Brake Offerings

Shown here is a 1970 Dodge Charger R/T. The standard engine on the R/T was the 375-hp 440-ci 4-barrel. For a few hundred dollars more, consumers could have the 425-hp 426-ci Hemi. For 1970, there was also the 390-hp 440-ci with a trio of Holley 2-barrels.

Dodge 330 1962–1964: Front and rear drum brakes were offered.

Dodge 440 1963–1964: Front and rear drum brakes were offered.

Dodge Challenger 1969–1974: Front disc brakes were standard.

Dodge Charger 1966–1975: Front disc brakes were an option from 1967.

Dodge Coronet 1965–1975: Front disc brakes were an option from 1967.

Dodge Dart 1959–1975: Front disc brakes were optional in 1965 and standard on the Swinger in 1970. They did not become standard on all models until 1976.

Dodge Lancer 1961–1962: Front and rear drum brakes were offered.

Dodge Polara 1962–1964: Front and rear drum brakes were offered.

Dodge Super Bee 1968–1971: Front and rear drum brakes were offered.

Plymouth Barracuda 1964–1974: Disc brakes were optional starting in 1965.

Plymouth Belvedere 1955–1970: Front and rear drums were offered. Front disc brakes were optional from 1967 on.

Plymouth Duster 1970–1975: Front disc brakes were standard on 318 and 340 models starting in 1973.

Plymouth Fury 1961–1964/1974–1975: Front and rear drum brakes were offered from 1961–1964. Front disc brakes were standard from 1974 on.

Plymouth GTX 1966–1971: Front and rear drum brakes were offered. Front disc brakes were optional from 1967 on.

Plymouth Road Runner 1968–1975: Front disc brakes were optional from 1968.

Plymouth Satellite 1964–1974: Front and rear drums were offered. Front disc brakes were optional from 1967 on.

Plymouth Savoy 1962–1964: Front and rear drum brakes were offered.

Plymouth Superbird 1970: Front disc brakes were offered.

Plymouth Valiant 1960–1975: Power front disc brakes were available in the Scamp package in 1974 and later. ∎

Ford did not offer hydraulic brakes until the 1940s, so many of the 1932 Roadsters seen today with hydraulic drum brakes are perfect examples of the earliest OEM-style brake swaps.

Hydraulic Brakes

About the same time, Malcolm Loughead (Lockheed Corporation) designed the first hydraulic braking system. Mechanical brakes, which were a simple design, required more effort from the driver, and unless the system was maintained frequently, the brakes did not apply pressure to all wheels evenly, causing control issues.

The Model A Duesenberg was the first production car to use four-wheel hydraulic brakes in 1921. Very few cars used the four-wheel hydraulic brakes in manufacturing until 1923. Chalmers began offering this as an option for the fairly steep price of $75, which is about $1,053 today.

Walter P. Chrysler, a product of the Chalmers company before starting his own car company, used the four-wheel hydraulic brakes based on the Chalmers system, but Chrysler's were fully redesigned. Incorporating rubber cup seals in place of the leaky rawhide seals that Lockheed used, the Chrysler hydraulic brakes were more dependable. Loughead allowed Chrysler to use his design as long as he was able to use Chrysler's improvements.

The new system was referred to as the Chrysler-Lockheed hydraulic brakes and was used in Chryslers from 1924 to 1962. Undeterred by the cost to make such a system, Buick and Cadillac also began to make four-wheel brakes standard equipment on their cars. Car builders that did not want to offer the four-wheel brakes made outrageous claims that they were unsafe. By the end of the decade, it was clear that four-wheel brakes were not only here to stay, they were the standard.

As hydraulic brakes continued to improve, more and more manufacturers opted to use the hydraulic brake system over the durable mechanical brakes. Chevrolet and Ford were

Strangely enough, mechanical brakes are still common on many muscle cars. Parking brake systems, such as this Wilwood brake system, still use brake shoes and cable actuation for the parking brake. Brake shoes work well in this fashion because they are only used to hold the car in one spot and not to slow the car down at speed.

Chrysler's Crown Imperial was always a top-of-the-line luxury car, but it could have been argued that it was an early entry into the muscle car market. Advances in power and braking made the Crown Imperial a favorite to many, but high cost and extravagant styling moved the marquee out of the muscle car arena before the movement even began. This 1957 example shows the tipping point when luxury won out over performance in the nameplate.

holdouts until Bendix, the company that supplied General Motors with mechanical brakes, bought out Lockheed and began manufacturing hydraulic brakes. General Motors then switched to hydraulic four-wheel brakes for all of its cars in the mid-1930s. Ford continued with mechanical brakes until the early 1940s, when it finally adopted the hydraulic brakes. Ford was the last automaker to do so.

Post-War Developments

Disc brake technology improved in large part due to the automotive industry borrowing designs from World War II aircraft. Chrysler's 1949 Crown Imperial and the 1950 Crosley Hotshot are the most notable of these examples.

Initially, the hydraulic brake master cylinders were a single-reservoir-type system. In the early 1960s, the hydraulic brakes and hydraulic clutch systems were operated from the same master cylinder, such as the one pictured. In the mid-1960s, the dual master cylinder appeared with two wheels operating from the front part of the master cylinder and the other two wheels operating from the rear portion of the master cylinder. The most common early dual systems were a split front/rear system. In 1967, American Motors Corporation (AMC) produced cars with a diagonal split system, where the right front and left rear are served by one actuating piston and the left front and the right rear are served by a second actuating piston. This system became the preferred split system in the 1970s.

Despite the improvements, disc brakes were still not as reliable and were considered too expensive to be an affordable upgrade. It would be another 20 years, at the end of the muscle car era, before disc brakes became standard equipment from manufacturers.

European cars were widely using disc brakes in the late 1950s, but American manufacturers were pushed into disc brake technology with 1967's Federal Motor Vehicle Safety Standard that set the stage for disc brakes on American cars. Disc brakes would wait, but the traditional drum brake technology continued to evolve.

Power-Assist Brakes and Self-Adjusting Brakes

Unbelievably, the first brake assist appeared in the Tincher automobile made in Chicago in 1903. The system employed a small compressor pump that helped stop the car, inflate tires if needed, and sound the whistle horn. Pierce-Arrow produced the 1928 models with a vacuum-operated power brake booster, borrowing from the aviation industry for its production car.

Other power-assist brake systems appeared here and there over the years, but after the war, power brakes were commonplace. Various vacuum systems were available through the 1950s from various manufacturers, including Bendix. The Bendix system was available on all GM cars but could also be found on Edsel, Lincoln, Mercury, Nash, and a few other brands. The Delco power booster system eventually took over as the system of choice at the end of the decade. A firewall-mounted power booster provided a true power assist, allowing the car to be smoothly brought to a stop without excessive pressure.

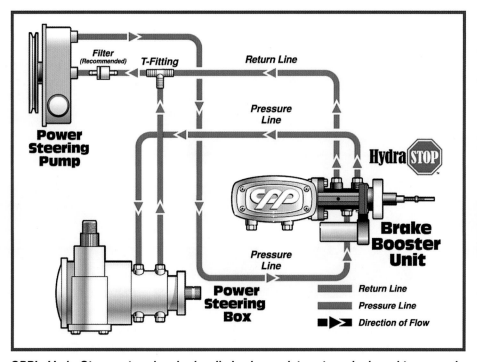

CPP's HydraStop system is a hydraulic brake assist system designed to upgrade manual or vacuum-assisted brakes with a compact hydraulic assist unit. This is especially helpful when engine vacuum is low and traditional power assist won't work correctly. (Illustration Courtesy Classic Performance Products Inc.)

The CPP HydraStop unit comes in a few different styles, but this Street Beast version is the most popular. The unit uses fluid pressure from the power steering system to assist in applying pressure to the master cylinder.

The main component in the self-adjusting brake system is the self-adjusting screw. The adjusting screw is basically a threaded device that extends and contracts. The head of the adjustment screw is a notched wheel with a cylindrical pin. The pin is capped with a washer and a slotted cap on each end. The slots fit into the brake shoes to add pressure as needed due to friction pad wear.

This is the basis for power-assist systems still used today.

Much like the power-assist brakes, self-adjusting brakes existed almost as early as drum brakes but not as frequently through the decades. First appearing on the 1925 Cole, the Indianapolis-based company specialized in luxury cars, but the 1925 model would be its last. Self-adjusting brakes would not return until after the war when Studebaker adapted a Wagner Electric unit to its cars. Slow to catch on, the self-adjusting drum brakes continued to be fitted to more vehicles in the 1960s.

Antilock Brakes

Antilock brake systems (ABS) may sound more like a modern invention, but nothing could be further from the truth. French aviation pioneer Gabriel Voisin, the creator of Europe's first engine-powered airplane and major manufacturer of military aircraft, developed the first antilock brakes.

Voisin became a manufacturer of luxury cars later in his career with a company he called Avions Voisin. Voisin first used the antilock brakes on aircraft in 1929. They were introduced in his automobiles shortly thereafter.

Mercedes-Benz debuted an electronic ABS in 1936, and the British Jensen sports cars used a similar basic electronic ABS in 1966. Other car manufacturers experimented with antilock systems with varied success until Ford hit upon the Sure-Track system in 1969 for the Thunderbird and Lincoln Mark III models. These systems were a Kelsey-Hayes antilock unit that included wheel sensors on each wheel that transmitted reference signals to a computer in the dash panel. There were some problems with the system, and it only controlled the rear wheels, but the theory was in place.

Chrysler and General Motors both offered ABS in 1971 as options. Ford joined the club in 1975 as options on its Lincoln Continental Mark II and the LTD Station Wagon. Antilock brakes became common-place in the late 1990s, and even work trucks were fitted with these handy safety devices. Modern vehicles use ABS integrated with long- and short-range radar that can bring a car to a stop even if the driver doesn't activate the brake pedal.

Theory of Braking Systems

Until the turn of the century, brake systems have not received the accolades that many of the other systems in automotive manufacturing have. Engines, transmissions, rear ends, wheels and tires, along with electrical and ignition systems have all earned their place in the limelight over the past century. Brakes, on the other hand, seem to have been more of a marketing item to the public than the actual applied science that the system is.

The theory of braking systems, most definitely a hard science, is not that complicated once some scientific terms are defined in common language.

Pascal's Law and Hydraulic Operation

Pascal's law, or Pascal's principle, was first stated by French scientist Blaise Pascal about fluid mechanics and is a fundamental law in physics. In the simplest terms, Pascal's principle describes that any pressure applied to a fluid inside a closed system will transmit that pressure equally in all directions throughout

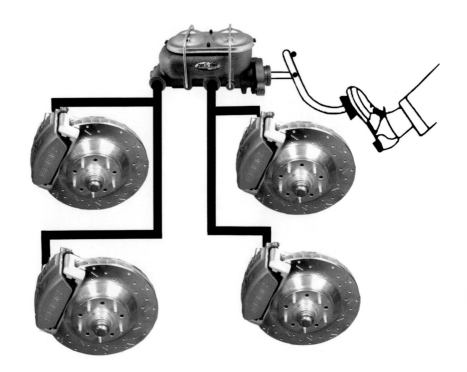

Brake systems operate by the pressure on one pedal applying pressure to all wheel cylinders. This is Pascal's law, which states that pressure applied to a fluid inside a closed system will transmit that pressure equally in all directions throughout the fluid.

The radial openings in most aftermarket rotors are channels or vents that go from the center of the rotor to the outside edge. These vents are often curved to draw hot air from the center of the rotor and route it to the outside, keeping the entire assembly cooler. Heat is the byproduct of the energy conversion created by braking.

the fluid. This is the very reason that hydraulic power works in everything from heavy equipment and lifts to automotive braking systems.

The brake master cylinder is filled with brake fluid. The master cylinder is equipped with a piston that actuates when the brake pedal is pressed. This forces fluid through the brake lines to the wheel cylinders or calipers equally. The small force applied at the brake pedal produces a larger force when all four wheels are involved.

Energy Conversion

To get a vehicle in motion, an internal combustion engine converts chemical energy (combustion) into motion energy. In physics, this energy of motion is called kinetic energy. A car in motion has a lot of kinetic energy and it takes a lot of chemical energy to get up to its velocity. Having gained that kinetic energy during acceleration, it will maintain that energy unless the speed changes.

It is important to remember that the amount of work done to create this kinetic energy is the same amount of work needed to decelerate from speed to a state of rest. Physics also tells us that the total energy of an object remains constant; energy cannot be created or destroyed but only transformed from one form to another. This is also known as the law of conservation of energy. The braking system uses friction to convert the kinetic energy into thermal energy.

There are many factors that combine to make this energy conversion happen, including the brake pedal ratio and brake line diameter. Without getting into too many details, here is a basic overview of how most brake systems work:

The vehicle operator steps on the brake pedal to slow down or stop. The brake pedal lever is connected to a rod that pushes a piston in the brake master cylinder. The master cylinder is filled with hydraulic fluid that gets pushed into the brake lines by the piston. The hydraulic fluid presses against pistons in slave cylinders located on each wheel. The slave cylinders actuate either brake shoes or caliper pads against the brake drum or brake rotor, applying enough force to stop the vehicle.

Here's where physics comes in. As the brake shoes or pads do their job, the kinetic energy of the vehicle is changed into heat. The biggest enemy to brake pads and brake shoes is heat. As the brake shoes or pads change the car's motion energy into heat, the brakes get hotter. If they get too hot, they won't work as well and will experience brake fade. It they get hot enough, the brakes

will lose their ability to stop the car because the shoes or pads lose their friction against the drum or rotor. The amount of heat generated by the brakes stopping a car at speed can hit 950°F or more.

To combat brake fade, manufacturers use different materials with higher heat resistance for different applications. These materials that resist degradation at high temperatures include composites, alloys, and even modern ceramics. Some of these materials, especially those used in the higher-performance brake sets, have brake rotors and pads that require some heat in them to have enough friction in the first place. When they are cool, the brakes don't have enough friction and won't stop the car as well. These types of brakes are used mostly in race cars and not on cars driven on the street. Using brakes kits with different materials in the rotors, pads, shoes, or drums

The brake pads ride very close to the rotor when they are not in actual contact. This leaves precious little room for cooling. Brake pad materials rely on mostly heat-resistant synthetic fibers to resist heating and brake fade. Ceramics and metal fibers from copper and other soft metals are also used in modern brake pads.

is one way to improve braking in muscle cars.

Most cars manufactured during the muscle car era were equipped with drum brakes on all four wheels. Modern braking systems tend to have disc brakes on the front and drum brakes on the rear. More-expensive models have four-wheel disc brakes. Disc brakes do a great job stopping a car and are simplistic in design and maintenance.

Another method to increase the braking in vintage muscle cars is to add disc brakes to the front wheels with parts intended for a similar-model car or from a kit designed by a manufacturer to work with the model of car you are performing the upgrade on. Since the front brakes do 75 to 90 percent of the braking, changing from drum brakes to disc brakes on the front is one of the most effective braking upgrades.

Stability, Steering, and Stopping Distance

Tires are literally where the rubber meets the road. Tires are the link between the vehicle and the road surface, and they are the final piece of the braking system. Tires actually stop the vehicle and play an important role in the change of speed and direction. Because these circular devices are involved in transmitting braking, motion, and lateral forces, any one of these forces can and will affect the others. The Motorcycle Safety Foundation (MSF) teaches its riders about this concept in what it calls "the traction pie."

The MSF has a traction pie graph that represents the total amount of traction that a tire can have. The pie-like segments define areas for acceleration force, braking force, turning, and a reserve. The four segments of the traction pie are ever changing, shrinking, or growing, depending on the action happening at the time. For example, under strong acceleration, that segment of the pie will be larger. The braking segment will shrink to nearly nothing, and turning will probably be somewhere in size between the acceleration and the braking segments. The reverse would be true if the condition was hard braking instead of hard acceleration.

The MSF goes on to explain that the total traction can be consumed by those three segments when they consume all the reserve. After that point, the tires will lose traction. In this explanation of traction, brakes play a key role in stability, steering, and stopping.

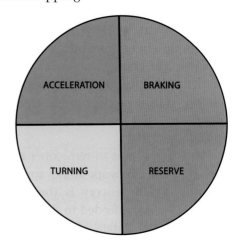

In a traction pie concept from the Motorcycle Safety Foundation (MSF), a circle that represents the total amount of traction available is divided by forces that consume that traction. Acceleration and braking take a large part of the available traction. Turning consumes some of the traction, and whatever is left over is held in reserve. According to the MSF, a reserve should always be maintained. If the reserve is fully consumed, a loss of traction will result in a skid or a spin.

In addition to the various brake components, aftermarket manufacturers often produce their own lines of spindles and steering arms too. Spindles can be purchased that raise or lower the ride height of a vehicle but keep the steering geometry correct.

Engineering Details of Braking Performance

The engineering behind brake performance is much deeper than most motorists realize. A great number of factors need to be considered when designing a brake system for a specific vehicle. The vehicle itself figures into these equations.

"The effectiveness of any brake system depends on factors like the weight of the car, braking force, and total braking surface area," said Mark Chichester of Master Power Brakes. "You have to factor in how efficiently the system converts wheel motion into heat and how efficiently the built-up heat is removed from the brake system. The buildup and dissipation of heat go a long way toward explaining the major differences between drum and disc brakes."

Drum brakes are at a clear disadvantage when it comes to dissipating heat. As drum brakes get used hard, the brakes fade because of excessive heat buildup in the drum. The drum absorbs heat until it reaches a saturation point and is unable to absorb additional heat.

With disc brake systems, the rotors are not confined in a tight space; they are exposed to the outside air that provides a cooling effect and helps combat brake fade. Most basic disc brake conversion kits have rotors that are made of cast iron.

Cast iron is inexpensive and has great wear properties. Cast iron is also heavy, so those enthusiasts looking to gain performance by losing weight may want to consider rotors made from other materials, such as ceramic composites. Kits with these ceramic composite brakes are engineered to be heat resistant and able to handle higher compressive loads at higher temperatures.

Force Conversions

To understand how the force from stepping on the brake pedal is converted into pressure at the brake's friction pad or shoe, some elements of the common components in the braking system must be explained.

The force of a driver stepping on a brake pedal to stop a car traveling at a high rate of speed would need

Heat is the enemy of brakes, and one of the key advantages to using disc brakes is that they are more effective in the heat due to their ability to shed heat better.

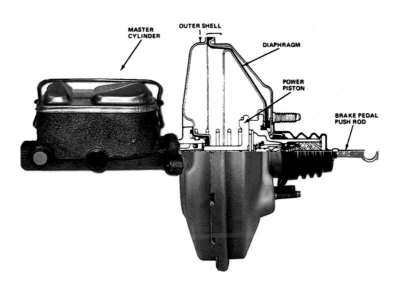

The vacuum-operated brake booster works today much as it did 50 years ago when muscle cars ruled the road. Drawing vacuum on the front of the diaphragm removes atmospheric pressure. The rear chamber is vented to the atmosphere and the pressure multiplies the force a driver applies with the brake pedal. This cutaway shows where the diaphragm placement in the brake booster is and how it works in relationship to the brake pedal actuator rod.

to be tremendous if the force wasn't multiplied. For instance, a young soccer mom in a 4,000-pound sport utility vehicle (SUV) running down the highway at 70 mph would need to use all 120 pounds of her body weight along with both feet standing on the brake pedal to even start slowing down the vehicle. Using that illustration, it is obvious that multiplying the force applied to the brake pedal is critical when engineering a braking system.

How the force is amplified from the driver's input into braking force is referred to as brake system gain. This gain is done mechanically and through vacuum assistance. It all starts with the driver stepping on the brake pedal. Without extra exertion, an average-size person delivers about 70 pounds of force on the brake pedal pad. The brake pedal is really a mechanical lever, and the positioning of the pedal pad in relationship to the mounting point (where the pedal pivots) and the point where the push-rod is attached to the master cylinder is how the force of the driver's action is multiplied.

How Upgrades Affect Vehicle Performance

There are several things to consider when planning a brake upgrade. These include gain, modulation, heat capacity, cooling rate, and weight.

Gain

Gain is a fancy term for multiplying the mechanical advantage. These gains can come from changing the pedal ratio, adding a brake booster, upgrading to a larger caliper piston size, or changing the size of the rotor. Larger discs allow for more brake torque because the brake pad will apply pressure at a larger radius, while larger caliper pistons (or more pistons) result in more area of applying a specific pressure.

Modulation

Brake modulation, in the simplest terms, is the ability to slow down or stop without locking up the brakes. Peak stopping power is just before the brakes lock up. The ability to control that peak range precisely is the goal of a well-designed brake system. Brake system upgrades usually have a better pedal feel and firmness with an improved ability to control brake lockup.

Heat Capacity (Thermal Mass)

Heat is the enemy of brakes. When temperatures get high enough, the brake pads start fading and eventually lose the capacity to work properly. Heat is frequently absorbed by the brake system components, which can be dissipated at a rate depending on the mass and material. Thermal mass or thermal capacity are terms often used to describe the ability of the brakes to shed heat without reaching temperatures that would interfere with proper braking. Modern aftermarket brake systems use materials and component designs that allow for higher heat capacity.

Cooling Rate

Upgraded brake systems usually have better cooling through material and venting design. Slotted and drilled rotors, curved cooling vanes in rotors, materials with better heat dissipation, and a larger surface area all factor into manufacturing modern aftermarket brake systems.

One of the quickest and easiest ways to improve gain in the braking system is to change the brake pedal. The braking ratio can be changed with an increase or decrease of distance between the pedal's hinge point and where the master cylinder piston connects to the pedal.

In addition, drum brakes are enclosed. All of the heat is trapped inside the drum. Disc brakes have rotors that are exposed to airflow and more efficient cooling.

Weight (Unsprung and Rotating)

Converting from drum brakes to disc brakes often results in a substantial weight reduction. Whenever there is a weight loss, two terms apply: sprung/unsprung weight and rotational weight.

Sprung weight is any portion of the car that is held up by the coil springs; the rest is unsprung weight. The largest part of a braking system (drums or discs and calipers) is unsprung weight. For performance, car builders try to minimize the unsprung weight because it hurts handling. This weight is supported by tires and shocks.

Rotational weight is any part that rotates when speed is accelerated or decelerated. It takes more horsepower to turn rotating weight and to decelerated rotating weight. Taking off the heavy drum brakes and installing lighter rotors helps minimize the amount of rotating mass. This is also an important factor when upgrading to aftermarket wheels. Increasing weight requires more horsepower to turn and more brake force to slow down.

Modern Braking Performance Versus High Performance

When it comes to selecting a disc brake conversion or improving to a higher-performance braking system, a few factors come into play. What are your plans? Will the car be used as a daily driver to enjoy driving back and forth to work and home, or will it be going to the track, doing some canyon carving, or hitting the autocross course regularly? As with almost anything else, the budget for it will likely play a large role in the decision.

If you are simply looking for an up-to-date brake system that is compatible with today's city traffic, or the budget is tight but you still want safe and confident braking, then an OEM-style replacement brake conversion kit is probably all you need. However, if you are hitting the track, a mid-level or high-performance kit will probably serve your needs better.

Evaluating an aftermarket brake system boils down to a few critical elements.

Larger Disc Radius: A larger disc radius allows for more brake torque. The brake pads will apply more pressure over a larger radius by virtue of being farther from the center of the wheel. Selecting the largest rotor that fits safely within the wheel is helpful for good braking force.

Caliper Piston Area: Selecting a kit with larger pistons or more pistons (increasing the piston area) allows the system to increase the brake force due to larger piston area. If the line pressure remains consistent, the increase in piston area means the applied force will increase.

When converting from factory-original drum brakes to aftermarket disc brakes, the differences are very noticeable. The weight difference is visually obvious.

In addition, the drum brake shoes are contained in the drum and shielded away from cooling airflow. Any debris from the shoes are also contained in the drum. Disc brake rotors and pads are open to the environment and make better use of cooling and cleaning.

Increasing Line Pressure: Increasing line pressure by adding a power booster or improved pedal ratio helps increase braking force.

Material Selection: Selecting brake pad and rotor material to improve the coefficient of friction between the pad and rotor can increase the braking force. There is a tradeoff when generating more friction, which is more heat. Larger rotors will help shed heat, especially if the rotors are designed with cooling in mind.

Rotor Design: In addition to larger rotors, cooling vents that allow for airflow through the center of the rotor greatly improve the ability to efficiently provide cooling and prevent brake fade. Slotted and drilled rotors assist by allowing gasses to escape and remove particles that are created by brake pads and rotors during braking.

The caliper piston area varies from manufacturer to manufacturer and even different-sized calipers can be found within the same manufacturer's line of products. This is a compact single-piston caliper from Wilwood Engineering. (Photo Courtesy Wilwood Engineering Inc.)

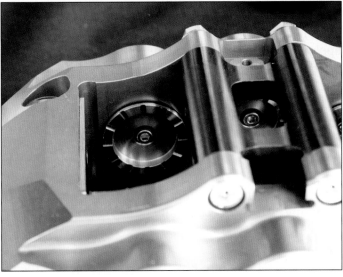

The research engineering and product development is very specific to different applications. Multi-piston calipers may even have different-sized pistons in the same caliper housing.

Piston area alone is not the only determining factor for which brake system is best for your application. Pad material, rotor radius, and construction all play a role.

A brake booster is designed to provide power assistance to the braking effort, meaning you do not have to put a lot of force on the brakes for them to actually operate and engage the rotors. The brake booster is located between the brake pedal and master cylinder and uses a vacuum to overcome the fluid pressure in the braking system. This is covered in detail in chapter 2.

Types of rotors, calipers, hubs, and brake pads have changed over the decades. Modern technology has affected the manufacturing process as well as the materials and design of these components to make them higher performing and more durable than ever before.

Some rotors are solid one-piece units, while others are multi-piece construction for strength and cooling properties featuring slotted and vented designs.

The rotor design, construction, and material are critical factors in a modern performance brake system. The Society of Automotive Engineers (SAE) maintains a specification for the manufacture of grey iron for various applications, including passenger cars.

Rotor hubs are often manufactured with slots in the hub to help with cooling without sacrificing strength or structural integrity in the component. This technology was not used in the muscle car era but is available in aftermarket brake kits now.

COMPONENTS AND THEIR FUNCTIONS

With the fundamentals of the hydraulic brake system understood, it's time to review the many components within the automotive braking system. Similar to the vehicle they're used to slow and stop, there are many variables, accessories, and styles of components used depending on the application.

As the majority of automotive brake systems operate on the same principles of hydraulic pressure and physics, many of these components are common to nearly any car on the street or track. Granted, advanced electronics have stepped into the braking performance world with anti-lock systems on newer vehicles, but we'll keep our focus on the braking systems used in the majority of hot rods, muscle cars, and road-course warriors being built and run on the track. Many of these components were lightly covered in chapter 1, but the following sections break them down in greater detail through a systematic approach.

Brake Pedal and Assembly

Since the braking process begins with your foot pressing the brake pedal, it is fitting to start our discussion there. The brake pedal assembly is one component that is probably taken for granted when a

Like engine parts, brake system components come in a lot of shapes and sizes, depending on your application and braking performance expectations.

The brake system starts with your foot pressing a pedal, so weigh your options for pedal position and movement along with how much pressure you're comfortable with providing.

brake system upgrade is planned, but it should certainly be considered and reviewed to see how it could be improved.

The pedal assembly acts as a simple lever. There is another rod connected to the lever that forces a pushrod into the master cylinder chamber to pressurize the brake system. The position and length of the pedal lever and its pivot point affect how much force is supplied to the master cylinder and how much force is required. It is also important to consider the location of the brake pedal in relation to the throttle and clutch pedals. Many older cars or trucks have quite a space between the pedals, which will not bode well in a performance application.

Depending on the goals for your car, a completely new brake pedal assembly may not be necessary, but when you're getting serious about performance and braking, many of the aftermarket assemblies will provide the strength and adjustments needed. There are assemblies that mount to the floor or the firewall and have adjustments to position each pedal exactly to fit your needs. Having the pedals closer together and on a single plane will provide a much better driving and braking experience.

Also, moving to a new pedal assembly provides more alternatives and solutions for mounting the master cylinder(s). Aftermarket pedals are designed to accept remote master cylinders or even dual units (one for the front, one for the rear) that provide increased adjustments for pedal feel and braking bias between the front and the rear. For those applications, an entire assembly for the throttle, brake, and clutch will be in your future and would be a wise investment.

Brake Fluid and Hydraulics

The brake system is like a mini hydraulic network with plumbing to each wheel running up to a common point: the master cylinder. The

Wilwood offers a list of pedal assemblies for street cars through sprint cars. This example is built with a clutch pedal and allows the master cylinders (hydraulic clutch too) to be mounted inside the firewall. (Photo Courtesy Wilwood Engineering Inc.)

brake pedal uses mechanical leverage to exert force onto the pushrod and piston of the master cylinder, which pressurizes the fluid in the lines and against the pistons of the calipers or wheel cylinders.

The small piston and area within the master cylinder can move a larger piston (like in the caliper) with more force, albeit a shorter distance. Think

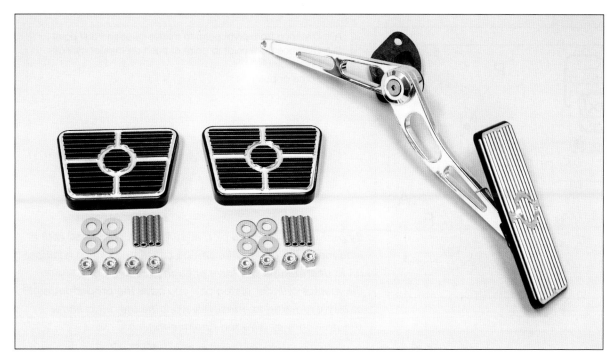

Pedals and pedal pads can dress up the interior and put your own personal touch in your pride and joy. This could be the perfect companion to a disc brake upgrade to your classic muscle car. This set is from Billet Specialties.

Pedal Pressure

Knowing the pedal ratio (mechanical leverage) of the brake lever will allow the amount of force required to activate the brakes to be increased or decreased. By varying the pedal ratio, the brake pressure can be adjusted without changing the amount of pressure applied by foot. The trade-off is that the amount of lever movement necessary will change.

To calculate the pedal ratio, measure the distance from the pivot point of the brake lever to the middle of the pedal push point and divide that by the distance from the pivot point to the pushrod connection (A / B = PR).

A: The length of the pivot point to the center of the pedal

B: The length of the pivot point to the master cylinder pushrod

PR: Pedal Ratio

Example: A is 5 inches, and B is 1 inch, so the ratio is 5:1.

By adjusting the lengths, the brake force can be increased/decreased without increasing the pedal feel/effort. The diagram illustrates the measurements and effects on the brake pressure. The catch here is that the amount of movement on the pedal will increase.

If you have a pedal ratio of 5:1 with 100 pounds of force acting on a master cylinder with a 1-inch stroke, the pedal pressure is 5 x 100 = 500 pounds, while the stroke is 5 inches. Stepping up to a 6-inch stroke will give you 600 pounds of pressure, but the stroke would be longer at 6 inches (6 x 1 = 6 inches).

Mark Chichester with Master Power Brakes explained the brake pedal ratio as a mechanical lever advantage. "If the overall length of the brake pedal is 12 inches and the distance between the pivot point and where the pushrod connects is 3 inches, the brake pedal ratio is 4:1. Anything between 4:1 and 5:1 is a perfect ratio for a power brake system. A manual brake system is better suited for a pedal ratio between 5:1 and 6:1. In the example above, the distance between the pivot point and where the pushrod connects would need to be changed to 2 inches for a 6:1 ratio."

The force multiplication of the pedal ratio can be calculated by multiplying the initial force by the ratio. For example, let's assume the average force of 70 pounds is applied to the brake pedal. Multiply that by 4 to get the total force for a 4:1 brake pedal ratio (70 x 4 = 280 pounds of output force). Likewise, a 6:1 ratio would result in 420 pounds of output force (70 x 6 = 420). The pivot point placement and master cylinder pushrod location in higher-ratio brake pedals tend to have longer pedal travel.

Chichester also mentioned some general rules that most designers adhere to: "Whether your vehicle has power or manual brakes, pedal ratio is important. If you are experiencing a hard pedal, you should check your pedal ratio if you have converted from the vehicle's original setup. As a general rule, your pedal ratio should not exceed 6:1 for manual brakes with a 1-inch bore master cylinder and 4:1 for power brakes with a $1^1/_8$-inch bore master cylinder." ∎

A = Distance from pivot point to middle of push / pull point
B = Distance from pivot to point of push on master cylinder
P = Pivot point
F = Force or push

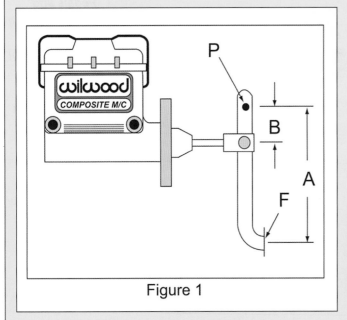

Figure 1

By performing a few quick measurements combined with a little math, the pedal ratio can be calculated, which is helpful to determine if you have enough pressure acting upon the master cylinder piston or if you have the proper amount of travel required to effectively work the master cylinder. (Photo Courtesy Wilwood Engineering Inc.)

of it like a floor jack and how big of a stroke is needed with the handle to move the lifting mechanism.

The fluid used in a brake system undergoes tremendous pressure and heat cycles. Like engine oils, there are several different grades of brake fluid to choose from to match your goals and driving conditions. The most common fluids are specified by the Department of Transportation: DOT3, DOT4, and DOT5.

DOT3 is the base fluid and is not as capable of performing in higher-performance applications compared to the DOT4 blend.

DOT4 brake fluid is considered a higher-performance brake fluid because of the addition of borate esters, which improve the dry and wet points of the fluid. While DOT4 brake fluids are more stable and have a higher boiling point initially, once the fluid begins to absorb water, its boiling point will fall off more rapidly than most DOT3 brake fluids.

Use care so the brake fluid is not exposed to open atmosphere where it can pull water molecules from the air. DOT4 brake fluids must have a minimum dry boiling point of 446°F (230°C) and a minimum wet boiling point of 311°F (155°C) by US Federal Motor Vehicle Safety Standards (FMVSS).

The dry boiling point of brake fluid is described as the boiling temperature of brake fluid from an unopened container. The wet boiling point refers to the brake fluid boiling point after it has absorbed 3.7 percent water by volume. Most experts estimate that brake fluids reach this point just past the two-year mark. This is why the experts recommend changing brake fluid every two years.

DOT5.1 brake fluids also have a

Brake Fluid Type	Composition	Dry Boil Temp	Wet Boil Temp
DOT3	Glycol based	401°F	284°F
DOT4	Glycol based	446°F	311°F
DOT5	Silicone	500°F	356°F
DOT5.1	Glycol based	518°F	374°F

The Department of Transportation rates brake fluid in several classifications; always check with a brake manufacturer for its recommendation. DOT3 provides the characteristics for most cars; for spirited performance and on-track days, DOT4 is recommended.

blend of ethyl glycol and borate ester, but this blend meets the standards of the silicone-based DOT5 brake fluid. In simple terms, the DOT5.1 brake fluid is a DOT4 fluid that meets the DOT5 standards. Because the blend is essentially the same, DOT5.1 and DOT3 and DOT4 brake fluids are compatible.

DOT5 is a silicone-based fluid which, while not designed for high-performance driving, is a favorite among hot rodders because it will not remove paint if it gets spilled or splashed compared to DOT3 and 4, which are highly corrosive to paints and coatings.

Brake fluid must hold its operating parameters through quite a few different requirements. It must have an extremely low freezing point as well as an extreme boiling point. During those varied operating parameters, it

must have a constant viscosity and not maintain its compressibility. Add to the list its ability to lubricate the moving components and prevent corrosion, it makes for a pretty tall order. Believe it or not, the fluid also needs to be able to absorb any moisture that collects in the system.

It's always a best practice to fill a fresh brake system with new brake fluid. A brake fluid canister that has been open on a shelf will absorb moisture in the air. By pouring it into an existing brake system, you would be introducing more moisture. It is important to note that mixing DOT3 and DOT4 fluids is acceptable. However, never mix a DOT5 synthetic fluid with a glycol-based fluid. Component deterioration as well as the transfer of pressure will not function as well when combined.

TBM Brakes offers a high-end brake fluid for the most severe applications. This DOT5.1 fluid is suitable for long races and whenever critical conditions are present. Rated at a 612°F dry boiling point, it has slow moisture absorption and is compatible with all DOT3 and 4 brake fluids.

Master Cylinder

The master cylinder is one of the most important components of your brake system and plays a direct role in the resulting pedal effort, modulation, and the overall braking effectiveness of the system. When selecting a master cylinder, it is highly advised to use the recommendation of the brake system manufacturer due to the number of variables in caliper, booster, or drum designs and fitments.

The master cylinder of the braking system is the heart of the system. It has a reservoir to hold the brake fluid and it converts the mechanical effort from the brake pedal into hydraulic pressure to activate the brake calipers or drums. To simplify its operation, inside the cylinder is a piston that is pushed through a bore by a pushrod connected to the brake pedal assembly. As the piston is pushed into the cylinder, it pressurizes the system with brake fluid.

Within the cylinder, there are small ports that direct the fluid to the proper brake circuit. This creates pressure that acts upon a slave cylinder (wheel cylinder or caliper piston), which in turn pushes the brake pad against the rotating drum or brake rotor.

Many older vehicles were equipped with a single-channel master cylinder, which should be one of the first items updated on any vehicle that will be driven. The reason is simple: safety. A single reservoir is responsible for maintaining both the front and rear brake circuits, and if one circuit is compromised, it will affect the operation of the other. For example, if a rear brake line fails, not only would the rear brakes be inoperative, the front brakes would also diminish! A

Upgrading to a dual reservoir in place of a single-chamber unit is an important upgrade. This example does not have any power assist and simply required a new line and proportioning valve to slow the application of the rear brakes. The bracket shown in the photo allows the master cylinder to be mounted under the floorboard, a common practice in street rods.

There is nothing good about a single-line master cylinder. If there is a leak in one of the four wheel cylinders or damage to a line occurs, the vehicle's overall braking capabilities will be lessened. Stepping up to a dual-port master cylinder that separates the front and rear brake circuits is a much safer system and should be high on the list of future upgrades.

single reservoir can easily be upgraded to a dual master cylinder.

A dual master cylinder, often referred to as tandem, splits the front and the rear system, which keeps the two systems separate to maintain braking function if one system fails.

These have two outlets, one for the rear with the other for the front.

For street applications, go with a tandem design that has separate outlets for the front brakes and the rear. When selecting a master cylinder, determine whether you plan

In a tandem master cylinder, brake fluid is secured in two independent reservoirs. If one brake circuit fails, the other will continue functioning properly. Notice the ports that direct fluid into the cylinder chamber.

A popular place to mount the master cylinder on street rods is to the chassis right under the driver-side floor pan. This bracket assembly is being fit on an early 1950s Chevy.

to run power assist or stick with manual brakes. There are a few typical bore sizes, such as 7/8-, 15/16-, or 1-inch diameters and the varying bore size will have an effect on the pedal feel.

A larger bore will create more displacement or volume but requires more pedal force, while a smaller bore will produce more pressure. There is no one guideline when selecting

a master cylinder because there are so many variables on each vehicle, such as the calipers, weight, suspension, and even seat position. Use components from a single source

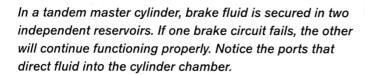

Selecting a Master Cylinder

Selecting the proper master cylinder for your application is key to the overall performance of the system and feel of the brake pedal. Review your goals with the brake manufacturer before making a choice.

Selecting a master cylinder is not only important for the operation of the brake system but it also affects the pedal feel. This is where knowing the pedal ratio and the force used comes into play. You may like a firm pedal feel, but what if you're building a street rod and your better half drives it, will they welcome the stiff pedal as well?

Keep in mind that a larger cylinder bore creates more fluid volume, while a smaller cylinder produces more pressure. If you're going to have a very short pedal ratio, a smaller cylinder may create a brake system with little feel or modulation. In fact, it will become more of an on/off feel with little in between. Conversely, a softer, longer pedal may be slow reacting and take too much movement to effectively slow the vehicle.

This is where it is important to discuss your plans and goals with the manufacturers, especially when it comes to the master cylinder. ■

since manufacturers design and engineer their products to work together.

Power Assist

In the brake system world, there are either manual brakes or power-assisted brakes. Manual brakes have a harder, definitely firm, pedal feel because you're dealing strictly with the mechanical contact and hydraulic force within the master cylinder and the geometry of the pedal and rod assembly.

Many original high-power muscle cars were ordered with manual brakes for simplicity and less weight (or had cams that were too big to make enough engine vacuum to support a booster). Older street rods also may choose the manual route simply due to the packaging under the hood. However, most rods these days (and even many muscle cars) are going with some form of power assist on their brake systems. Remember, disc brake systems require more pressure than drums (approximately 900 to 1,200 psi) to function as designed, so in the majority of cases, assist is a nice feature.

The most common form of adding power assist to the brake system is through a vacuum-operated booster. Vacuum boosters are available in a number of diameters and sizes to fit different applications.

There are two main systems for power brakes: hydraulic assist or with a vacuum booster. There are also electric vacuum motors available, but not many of those have been seen in the field yet. The most typical design is through a vacuum booster.

Vacuum Booster

A vacuum booster is a round, dish-like assembly that mounts between the master cylinder and the pedal assembly. It connects directly to an engine vacuum source and uses the vacuum and atmospheric pressure to help move the pushrod into the master cylinder.

Most brake companies specify that an engine needs to be able to create a minimum of 17 inches (or more) of vacuum for a stock-style brake booster to work at peak efficiency. This is typically a conservative recommendation, and many systems will work effectively with engine vacuum at levels of 12 inches for normal street operation.

Where lower vacuum causes a problem is during panic braking or an emergency stop situation. Additional effort may be required under those circumstances. Depending on the driver, this may exceed the ability of the driver to supply that extra effort.

When shopping for a booster, the customer will be asked about his or her engine's vacuum capability, the type of brake system being run, as well as if a single- or dual-diaphragm booster will be used. The customer should also consider any space containments for the diameter of the booster. Smaller boosters may fit better, but they require a stronger vacuum signal from the engine compared to their larger-diameter counterparts.

This booster and master cylinder assembly from Classic Performance Products is supplied as one matched unit for a specific application. This system, including the booster, master cylinder, and combination valve, is installed on a mid-1960s Chevrolet pickup.

A single-diaphragm booster works well with drum or disc/drum systems, but for four-wheel discs, a brake booster with a dual diaphragm should be used for the increased demand. Single-diaphragm brake boosters can provide as much as 950 psi, whereas the dual-diaphragm brake boosters produce more than the 1,000 psi typically required to operate four-wheel disc brakes. Dual-diaphragm brake boosters usually give extra braking even when the vacuum from the intake manifold is low.

Hydraulic Brake Assist

So, what do you do if your engine has a bit more power with a *thumpity-thump* cam grind that just doesn't make much vacuum? If you have power steering, there

COMPONENTS AND THEIR FUNCTIONS

is an alternative power-assist brake system that operates from hydraulic pressure rather than vacuum to assist in applying the brakes.

These systems were originally used on vehicles with diesel engines but have made their way into the hot rod world as an optional source for power-assist braking. The only sticking point is that you need to be running power steering because that's where the hydraulic pressure comes from. I am not aware of any kits that include a pump, but a pump can be purchased and a power steering deletion added so that it is a pump for the brake assist only.

A hydraulic brake assist system uses an assembly that looks like an extension of the master cylinder and mounts in place of the booster. Typically, the unit is about the same length as a large vacuum system and smaller in diameter. A low-pressure return line to the pump as well as two high-pressure lines need to be routed to the unit with one going to the gearbox and one coming from the power steering pump.

The benefit of hydraulic power assist is not having to make room for an unsightly (and in most cases, rather large) booster assembly. Conversely, installing a hydraulic-assist setup will require high-pressure hoses and fittings.

A hydraulic brake boost system has been employed on this 1936 Chevy chassis. Braking assistance will be added via hydraulic pressure from the power steering pump. The unit is not much longer than a vacuum booster.

Electric Assist

A modern take on power-assist brakes can also be achieved through an electric motor. There are specific vacuum motors available that operate on 12 volts. The system, offered through Speedway Motors, supplies up to 20 inches of vacuum and even has an adjustable switch allowing for the pump to cycle while maintaining the proper boost vacuum.

An alternative to a vacuum power assist is achieved by plumbing into the power steering system and incorporating the assist from hydraulic pressure. CPP offers its HydraStop system that will effectively provide the assist you need if your engine doesn't produce enough vacuum. The company even has a polished/chrome kit called the Show Stopper.

There are even electric power-assist systems available. This kit from Speedway Motors consists of a small 12-volt DC motor that will provide vacuum to a booster assembly if the engine cannot create the required vacuum needed due to a larger cam profile. (Photo Courtesy Speedway Motors)

Brake Lines

The brake system only begins with the master cylinder and fluid. Obviously, you need to plumb a network of lines and hoses to transfer the hydraulic pressure to each wheel. This is achieved through brake lines and hoses.

Hard lines are used to connect the master cylinder and run nearly the length of the vehicle to each wheel (with a junction block or metering valve inline). In the front, the hard line is generally run as close as possible to the wheel, where a flexible line comes into play to make up for suspension and steering movement.

Hard lines used are typically 3/16-inch steel tubing. Stainless steel tubing is also used, and many brake manufacturers offer tubing that is easy to bend without kinking or

MUSCLE CAR BRAKE UPGRADES: HOW TO DESIGN, SELECT, AND INSTALL   35

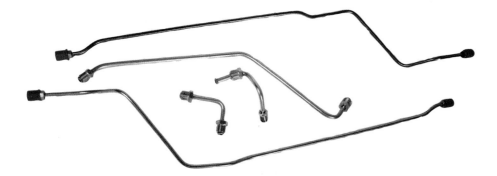

The hard line used for plumbing the brake system is typically 3/16-inch steel or stainless steel line. Many aftermarket companies offer steel-braided flex lines in a number of lengths, which are more durable than OEM replacement rubber hoses.

When building brake hard lines, a handheld bending tool will ensure smooth, kink-free bends around the chassis. Always secure the brake lines to the chassis to prevent vibrations or the chance of road debris pulling on a line.

A flex line is required to plumb the brake system to any wheel that turns or moves due to suspension travel. Flex lines are available in a number of lengths for different applications.

losing its form. All tubing must be resistant to corrosion and should be easy to flare and bend. It is also important to secure the hard lines to the chassis and solid mounting points to prevent them from snagging on road debris or from simply vibrating to the point of fatigue.

Up front, a flexible line will cover the area from the chassis to the caliper, allowing for movement with the suspension travel and turning of the wheels. In the rear, a single flexible line will generally be connected from the hard line at the center of the vehicle and connect to another hard line mounted to a live rear axle through a junction block to tee off into both sides.

When installing flex lines on a new or custom application, be sure to cycle the suspension and steering through their complete motion to ensure that the flexible line you are using is the proper length to reach the connections without being stretched or pulled taut.

Brake Valves

Depending on the application, there are several different accessory valves that mount inline of the brake plumbing to ensure the best operation and application of the front and rear brakes. Some of these components are similar in their operation with the goal of controlling the pressure and when it activates the different brake circuits.

Metering Valve

A metering valve is used on vehicles with front discs and rear drums and is tasked with equalizing the pressure between the front and the

A metering valve is required with disc/drum combinations to activate the rear brakes moments prior to the front. Note how the rear brake line (on the front of the master cylinder) routes to a metering valve before going to the rear drum brakes.

rear. In theory, the rear brakes should be energized before the front discs because of the inherent tendencies of the rear drum brake's spring and mechanical linkage design. This sequence of pressurizing the rear brakes first is done to prevent the car from dipping excessively in the front or locking up the front wheels first.

Proportioning Valve

A proportioning valve is used with disc or drum systems and is primarily installed inline on the rear brake line circuit. Its goal is to control or limit the rate of pressure increase at the rear wheels. By limiting, or at least slowing, the pressure rise, the valve will prevent the rear wheels from locking up under hard braking to compensate for weight transfer.

Some proportioning valves are preset, but there are also many adjustable versions that let you fine-tune the bias delay for your vehicle and driving characteristics.

Combination Valve

There is also a valve that combines the functions of a metering valve and a proportioning valve called a combination valve. Another common feature found in a combination valve is a port for a brake warning light or brake switch. A combination valve is primarily used in OEM and stock brake systems, so it will be designed exclusively for a specific brake system, drive, and vehicle weight. For performance applications, using a separate valve is the ideal way to go for optimum tuning per vehicle.

Residual Valves

In hot rodding, a common location for the master cylinder and booster assembly is under the driver's floor and mounted right to the chassis. This cleans up the engine compartment, and in many instances, it's simply the best location due to space constraints. However, when the master cylinder is located lower than the brake calipers or wheel cylinders, a residual valve in the brake lines must be installed.

The residual valve is a small inline device that prevents the fluid from the calipers and higher lines siphoning back down into the master cylinder. There are typically two different residual valves: 2 psi and 10 psi.

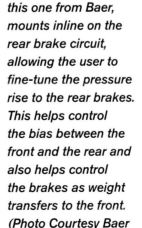

A combination valve is exactly as the name implies. It will be preset from the factory to the requirements of a specific-weight vehicle and application to control the brake bias, and this one has a port for a brake light switch or dash light. (Photo Courtesy Master Power Brakes)

An adjustable proportioning valve, such as this one from Baer, mounts inline on the rear brake circuit, allowing the user to fine-tune the pressure rise to the rear brakes. This helps control the bias between the front and the rear and also helps control the brakes as weight transfers to the front. (Photo Courtesy Baer Brakes)

If the master cylinder is mounted below the height of the caliper or wheel cylinders, a residual valve should be installed inline to prevent the fluid from syphoning down and to the master cylinder. Discs require a 2-psi valve, while a 10-psi valve is used for drums. (Photo Courtesy Speedway Motors)

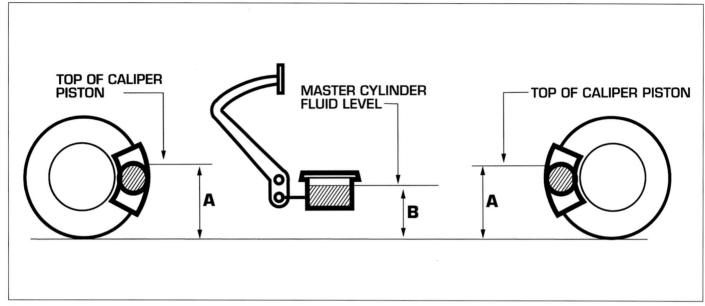

When the master cylinder is mounted on the chassis, which is typical on many street rod builds, there is a chance that fluid could syphon back down and into the master cylinder, causing a soft pedal or leaks. A residual valve should be installed on the front and rear lines. (Graph Courtesy Todd Ryden)

For a disc brake circuit, the 2-psi valve is used and keeps the fluid from draining back to the master cylinder. It also maintains pressure in the brake line to prevent excessive pedal travel or having to pump the pedal a couple times to have full braking capabilities.

A 10-psi valve is required on drum brake setups, unless the master cylinder already has one built in. The valve also protects the hydraulic system from air weeping in through the wheel cylinder seals, and like the smaller pressure valve, it helps keep pressure in the circuit to prevent a spongy-feeling brake pedal.

Master Cylinder with Built-In Residual Valve

Some factory-style master cylinders were built with a residual valve built into the assembly. But how can you tell?

The easiest way to determine if your master cylinder is equipped is to take a straightened paper clip and poke it into the brake line inlet on the master cylinder. If it slides in and bottoms out firmly, there's no valve. However, if it feels spongy or moves a little bit, there's a residual valve built in.

Even if the master cylinder is equipped with the valve, there will be no repercussion from installing one on the line down on the chassis. ■

To determine if your master cylinder has a residual valve, push a paper clip inside the outlet ports. If it bottoms out solidly, no valve. If it stops and gives a little, there's already a built-in residual valve and one will not need to be installed down the line.

In 1940, Ford introduced its first hydraulic brake system; since then, not a lot has changed. The wheel cylinder is on top, you can see the drum, the shoes, and the hardware in this original cutaway that Ford used as a promotional vehicle. It's important to note that these systems are not self-adjusting and require maintenance for the best stopping results.

This is the driver-side brake assembly on a 1969 Dodge Dart. Note the larger rear (secondary) brake shoe lining compared to the front shoe. The rear shoe is forced into the rotating drum by the front shoe so that it takes the brunt of the pressure during stopping.

Types of Automotive Hydraulic Brakes

The most commonly used forms of brake systems are drums and discs. Drums were the norm on all four corners through the late 1960s when discs started to become standard on the front wheels, creating a disc/drum combination.

There were options that could be checked off at the dealer to get a pony car fit with four-wheel disc brakes. These systems were a pricey addition at the time and were primarily installed on higher-end cars that were going to be seeing road-course miles and competition use.

Today's new cars are fit with disc brakes all around for good reasons. For the OEMs, there are fewer parts with disc setups, and for performance, the clamping force of a caliper gripping the rotor is much

more effective than a drum with two shoes pushing outward into the spinning drum.

Disc brakes are also much more efficient at dissipating the heat created to slow the kinetic energy, resulting in more consistent braking, especially under extreme braking. This is why drum brakes start to fade under hard-braking conditions.

A properly set up drum/disc braking system on a classic or hot rod is going to deliver safe, solid, and secure braking abilities for many enthusiasts and vehicles. However, if you're looking for better, repeatable braking performance, four-wheel discs are the way to go. Better yet is that there are many more options these days for bolt-on-style systems that will work with many different stock wheel combinations.

First, let's review the two systems in more detail to understand their function, abilities, and limitations.

Drum Brakes

Drum brakes have been around for many decades, but they are not considered a simple device or setup. In essence, a drum brake assembly includes the brake drum, a hydraulic wheel cylinder, a backing plate, brake shoes, and a number of retainers, springs, and levers to control the retraction and adjustment of the drum brake mechanism.

Wheel Cylinder

The wheel cylinder is part of the hydraulic system. Its housing connects directly to the brake line and directs the fluid to two opposing cylinders with pistons that are responsible for pushing the two brake shoes out and into the rotating brake drum. The cylinder also has an internal spring and seals (sometimes referred to as a cup) to keep fluid from leaking around the

The wheel cylinder of a drum brake system is mounted atop the backing plate and guides the hydraulic action to the two opposing pistons to push the shoes out toward the drum surface.

To keep the brake-pedal feel consistent over time, drum brakes are self-adjusting to compensate as the shoes and the drum surfaces wear. When the car is backing up and the brakes are applied, the small lever will click on the sprocket, which turns the adjusting screw out.

pistons, as well as a dust boot. In most cases, the pistons push an external rod that makes contact with the shoes and pushes them outward.

The wheel cylinder mounts to a backing plate that bolts to the axle or spindle. The backing plate also has mounting points for the two-shoe hold-down assemblies.

Brake Shoes

Brake shoes are rounded metal assemblies that secure a friction material. The friction compound is installed with rivets, a bonding adhesive, or both. It is important to note that the shoes are different in the length of the friction compound installed. They are identified as a primary and secondary shoe; the secondary shoe has a larger area of braking compound. The extra material is there due to the rotation of the wheel and the way the pads are pushed and pulled into the drum.

As the primary shoe makes contact with the rotating drum, it is pulled into the drum through friction. This self-energizing is referred to as "the servo action," which multiplies

the hydraulic force as the shoes pull harder against the rotating drum. In turn, the front shoe transfers pressure to the secondary shoe by pushing against the connecting adjustment screw, resulting in the secondary shoe applying more pressure; hence, it has a larger amount of friction material.

Drum Brake Adjusters

At the bottom of the drum brake assembly there is a device called an adjuster that is mounted between the two shoes. This screw-type adjusting device pushes the shoes out toward the drum as the linings wear over time.

The automatic adjustment occurs when the car is moving backward and the brakes are applied. There is a series of movements that activates a lever against a small sprocket-like wheel on the screw adjuster. This motion rotates the screw outward, which pushes the shoes out toward the drum to compensate for both drum and lining wear. It is important to disassemble, clean, and lube the screw adjuster and reset the assembly when replacing the brake shoes.

Brake Drum

The drum is essentially a round cover made of steel (in most cases) with a smooth machined surface inside where the brake shoes make contact to slow the wheel. The drum slides over the wheel studs and axle flange and is held secure with the wheel's lug nuts. Over time, the drum surface will wear and eventually need to be replaced.

Most brake drums are heavy assemblies made of steel or cast iron. These drums were prone to fade due to the heat that was held within the drum itself.

Disc Brakes

Disc brakes have fewer parts and are actually more effective at braking than drums. The components that make up a disc brake assembly include a rotor, a caliper, and brake pads. The rotor assembly bolts over the wheel studs or is part of the wheel hub assembly. The caliper is mounted over the rotor, and when hydraulic pressure is created, a piston (or pistons) pushes the pads out, creating a clamping force on the spinning rotor.

Calipers

In its simplest form, the brake caliper has a fluid reservoir along with a piston, a seal, and a dust cover. Most factory brake calipers feature a single-piston assembly on the inside of the brake rotor. The piston pushes the internal brake pad out toward the spinning rotor. The pad on the outer side of the caliper can be considered as a slave pad and is pulled into the rotor to clamp down.

Single-piston calipers are an effective and inexpensive system for OEM applications. The calipers are affixed to a bracket with two bolts through bushings or sleeves that allow the caliper to move (float) as the pads and rotor wear.

In performance applications, there are two or more pistons working to push the brake pads into the rotor surface. Generally, each side of the caliper has the same number of pistons on each side of the caliper. The increased number of pistons on both sides of the caliper adds strength to press the larger pads against the rotor. These calipers are retained securely to a solid mount rather than through a floating-pin assembly, such as an OEM or single-piston caliper.

Brake Pads

Pads consist of a steel backing plate with a lining compound mounted to it. The pads generally clip into the caliper or into the piston. In some cases, a small metal spring clip works as an anti-rattle device to squelch any vibration noise caused by the pads moving or vibrating in their mount.

Disc brakes consist of a brake rotor that can be part of the wheel hub or a separate component. These are generally called "one-piece" and "two-piece" rotors.

This OEM-style caliper has one large piston that pushes the internal pad into the rotor. As contact is made, the outer pad is drawn in. Also note the two mounting pins installed through bushings, allowing the caliper to float.

This is one side of a Baer six-piston caliper. The opposing side also has three pistons to equalize the pressure being applied on both sides of the rotor.

Slots and Drilling of the Rotor

When looking for rotors, options are available, such as slotted or cross-drilled rotors. There has been quite a bit of discussion on this topic, and today, both cross-drilled rotors and slotted rotors seem to serve more of an aesthetic purpose rather than giving a cooling or performance benefit.

When brake pads were made of primarily asbestos and other compounds, the pads would glaze over, resulting in a reduction in friction. The slots in the rotor would help deglaze the pads, and they still do to a certain extent today. Also, back with these asbestos-based pads, at extreme temperatures the bonding agents within the pads would begin to break down and release gasses, which is known as outgassing. There would still be a firm pedal, but the braking effectiveness would decrease. The drilled holes in the rotor would provide a manner to help the gasses escape.

Today, however, outgassing is a thing of the past thanks to advanced materials and technology in pad materials and compounds. Under certain conditions, slotting or drilling the rotor can provide a benefit and keep the rotor and pad clean. However, slotting the rotors seems to be the best option. Drilled rotors are more susceptible to cracking in higher-end applications. For street cars, even with a little track time now and then, they'll look good and hold up. ∎

Cross-drilled rotors may provide a performance look to your car, but under heavy-duty applications, cracking and failures can occur. For mild use, they will hold up just fine. The slots in the rotor will help clean any glazing material during heavy-duty use.

Rotor

The rotor, sometimes called the disc, is generally made of steel or cast iron for street car applications and has two parallel, smooth, flat surfaces where the brake pads make contact. Racing applications get into aluminum, titanium, and mixed alloys. Depending on the application, the rotor could also be integral to the wheel hub; however, in most performance applications they are separate pieces.

Many OEM rotors are solid pieces, while performance models are made with vents between the two surfaces. These vents have ribs that help dissipate the heat and circulate air across the rotor's internal surfaces.

Modern rotor technology includes a variety of different materials that were not available when American muscle cars were manufactured. Rotors such as titanium and carbon ceramic are available for special applications. This photo shows a carbon-ceramic rotor that is used on a professional autocross competition car.

Brake pads and shoes come in a number of sizes and shapes, and so does the friction material. Depending on your driving style, pads are made for racing, mild performance, or average street use.

Some rear disc brake kits use a lever assembly to activate the caliper mechanically for use as a parking brake. The parking brake cable is connected to a spring-loaded lever on this caliper from Stainless Steel Brakes Corporation.

Brake Lining Materials

The material and compounds that make up the pad and friction material of brake shoes and pads are numerous and can get confusing. Manufacturers and brake companies with their own offerings like to keep their compound recipes close to their chest and will help guide you with any recommendations.

Decades ago, asbestos was the number one source for braking materials, but we all know where that has gone. Today's pads consist of a number of different organic materials that are bonded through pressure and secured with an adhesive. There can also be a degree of metal particles included as well as ceramic materials.

Before selecting a pad for your application, the first step is to know what you plan to do with your vehicle: Is it going to be a good-handling street car with spirited driving, or will it see laps on an autocross track every couple of weeks? Do you plan to tow a trailer or carry heavy loads often?

There are mild, inexpensive pads made for daily driving or more aggressive compounds that require higher temperatures for optimum braking. Also, some materials may produce more noise, squeaks, or a thin, gripping noise that is more audible during stop-and-go street driving and could become an annoyance for daily driving.

Several characteristics are required of a friction material compound: the ability to resist fading, recovery from increased temperatures and repeated application, resistance to water, and the pad's service life compared to that of the rotor.

In your search for brake pads, there are three main categories: organic, semimetallic, and ceramic. Organic pads provide adequate braking for street cars but tend to expire sooner and produce a considerable amount of dust.

Semimetallic compounds are resistant to fade and last longer but require more hydraulic force. This added force is not friendly to the rotors or drums.

There are also metallic compounds that are generally reserved for racing. These can be loud and need a lot of force as well. The other alternative is ceramic compounds that still have a touch of metallic particles mixed in. Ceramic pads deliver a compromise with strong durability combined with resistance to fade.

Mounting a hydraulic switch for the brake light circuit is the best way to go when the brake pedal assembly has been replaced. When the switch senses a small rise in pressure, the contacts are closed to activate the brake lights.

An internal-shoe parking brake kit is another way to have a parking brake on a rear-disc application. The backing plate secures a pair of mini brake shoes that are lever activated and lock inside the two-piece rotor hat from Baer.

Parking Brake

A parking brake provides a mechanical method of applying the rear brakes while the car is parked. This is generally accomplished mechanically rather than hydraulically. There is typically a hand- or foot-actuated lever that pulls on a heavy-duty mechanical cable that pulls on another cable(s) to activate the rear brakes.

A parking brake is an important part of a brake system and is often overlooked when it comes to building a brake system on a classic car. In fact, an operational parking brake is just one of the many items checked by the National Street Rod Association (NSRA) to achieve its safety verification. Not only that, but many state vehicle inspections require a parking brake as well.

In stock rear drum applications, the parking brake cable pulls on another cable that actuates a mechanical lever that pushes the stock shoes out to hold the cable. For rear disc brakes, there are a few different techniques used to activate the parking brake.

Some aftermarket calipers are equipped with a parking brake lever that rotates a thrust-screw mechanism that pushes the caliper piston out to act as a parking brake. Another alternative that is offered is to have a small set of brake shoes that are secured to the backing plate of the rear brake assembly. These little shoes are controlled only by a lever and reside inside the hat of a two-piece rotor. This hat assembly acts as a drum, and when the lever is pulled, the brake shoes are pushed out and stop the wheels from turning.

All of the aftermarket brake companies offer parking brakes to complement their rear brake kits.

Regardless of the parking brake system that you select, if you drive your car on the street, install a parking brake!

Brake Light Switches

A brake light switch is needed in any brake system to operate the rear brake lights. When working on more of a G-machine muscle car and using the factory brake pedal assembly, retain the spring-loaded switch that is mounted under the dash and to the pedal assembly.

For custom setups, there are also hydraulically operated switches that activate the brake light circuit when pressure is sensed. These can easily be installed inline on the rear brake line with a junction block or in a combination valve with an open port for the switch. These switches only need to sense about 25 psi to close and activate the brake lights.

GENERAL BRAKE UPGRADE OVERVIEW

You don't need to go fast in a straight line to understand how important brakes are in classic muscle cars. Simply driving in congested traffic on today's highways are proof that disc brake upgrades are not only desired but a necessity.

Jousting for lane positions with much lighter modern cars equipped with high-performance brake systems puts a classic muscle car at a severe and unhealthy disadvantage. Even if you have no intention of putting your classic on an autocross course,

on a drag strip, or in a street race, a conversion from drum brakes to disc brakes is a wise move not only for you and your family but for others on the road as well.

Once the upgrade to performance braking has been decided, a few more decisions need to be made. Do you convert the front drum brakes to a disc brake system and leave drums on the rear? Perhaps you are looking to do some autocross events and want to upgrade the front and rear to disc brakes. Maybe you want to take

your car to some car show where you want to compete for a builder's award. More often than not, vintage muscle car owners simply want to perform a budget disc brake upgrade for their daily driver.

OEM Conversions

One of the first considerations in any upgrade is budget. How much do you want to spend on your brake system upgrade? Partial kits, such as a front brake upgrade, can range from

Autocrossing has become a very popular sport with enthusiasts. Using street cars that are often daily drivers with performance upgrades, the barriers to entry are low. Despite the lower speeds in competition, these street cars are on the gas and the brakes hard during this fast-paced competition.

The most common muscle car brake upgrade attempted by home garage builders is the OEM-style drum-to-disc replacement kit, such as this one from Classic Performance Products (CPP). CPP manufactures a full line of brake and suspension components for Ford, General Motors, and Mopar cars.

$600 to thousands, depending on the caliber and performance level of the components. Fortunately for car enthusiasts, most muscle cars made in the 1960s and early 1970s had very few variations within the nameplates. This means that special-option muscle cars with front disc brakes may be available in wrecking yards or replacement parts can be found off-the-shelf.

For example, GM's Chevelle and Malibu models were manufactured with the same style of brake master cylinders and even rotors were the same size from 1964 to 1969. Very few of these cars were built with front-wheel disc brakes. Hunting through wrecking yards for these rare cars will probably not result in much gain, but OEM replacement parts are affordable from several sources.

Even if you were to find the parts you need, the best of 1960s brake technology was mediocre at best. Brakes were not huge considerations in automotive engineering in the muscle car era. Tires and brake pad material were limiting factors. Fifty-year-old

Many manufacturers use GM factory C5 Corvette calipers in their brake kits for the single-piston, sliding-type caliper. This is not true of the CPP calipers that use 52-mm pistons.

The C5 Corvette calipers use a 40-mm piston. CPP's calipers also have larger pad surfaces that the company says offer nearly 50 percent more stopping power than the C5 calipers. Price-wise, the CPP calipers cost far less than a factory C5 Corvette caliper; plus, they have iron bodies that are more rigid, resulting in a firmer pedal.

technology is still not going to be safe on today's highways surrounded by vehicles with present-day stopping power.

Researching and finding a source for OEM-type disc brake conversions could possibly lower the overall cost of an upgrade, providing you are willing to spend the time to find the most cost-efficient components, but the project will most likely be complex.

OEM parts are usually readily available at your local parts store or Amazon. However, there is also a good possibility that you may need more components in an OEM-type conversion, such as different spindles, brake pedal assemblies, power boosters, combination valves, lines, etc.

Aftermarket Conversions

Fortunately for muscle car enthusiasts, a number of aftermarket brake companies make brake kits for almost every possible car and application. Many of these are plug and play or bolt on and go.

Companies such as Baer Brakes, Classic Performance Products, Master Power Brakes, Stainless Steel Brakes Corporation, and Wilwood have spent considerable time and resources developing brake kits that are simpler than trying to piece together individual components, and in most cases they are more economical as well.

Performance braking is more than just brakes. For the best braking function, the builder must also consider

While many consider this a budget-minded rotor, there are design features that make it higher performance than anything that was factory stock in the 1960s. This CPP rotor is cross-drilled, gas slotted, and zinc washed for heat transfer and durability.

Even the best disc systems of the late 1960s and 1970s left a lot to be desired. This technology and the materials are roughly 50 years old. A lot has changed in the past five decades. There is an entire industry built around aftermarket brake systems now.

Automotive brakes have become specialized to the point that every brake manufacturer has several lines of products. Depending on what the enthusiast is trying to achieve, there is a brake system dedicated to helping with that goal.

Prior to installing the brake kit onto the vehicle, put the rotor and hub together and check the fit inside the wheel you plan on using. Check for clearance. If it doesn't have enough clearance, you can send it back because technically, it hasn't been installed on the car.

The only drawback to big brake kits is that the rotor size forces the car's owner to use a larger wheel for clearance. Big brake kits require larger-diameter disc brake–type wheels. In this case, CPP's 13-inch kit requires 17-inch wheels to operate properly.

tires, suspension, wheelbase, and driving style. To get the maximum braking potential, low center of gravity, proper rear weight bias, and corner weight balance should be optimized.

Wheel Fit and Tires

Brake expert Bill Fowler, a former vice president of development at Baer Brakes, helped define the decision-making process.

"The first real questions to answer are: What are your intensions with the car, and what wheel and tire package will you be using?" Tires are a huge consideration because this is actually where the braking happens. The brakes slow the rotation of the tires and the braking ability of the tires is dependent on the tire compound.

"The most critical factor is the size of the wheel," Fowler added. "Even when the manufacturers began offering the single-piston front calipers on muscle cars, wheel size constraints left the engineers using smaller calipers so the braking force did not have an immediate impact."

Most early muscle cars from the 1960s and early 1970s were produced with 14-inch wheels. Using these stock wheels minimizes the size of caliper that can fit inside the wheel. Caliper size is directly proportionate to braking force.

"It's all about leverage," said Fowler, "like a larger-diameter steering wheel, or the difference between a 3/8-inch drive ratchet and a 1/2-inch drive ratchet."

According to most of the leading brake experts in the industry, a 15-inch tire is the minimum size for any performance braking system on muscle cars. Backspacing, tire tallness, diameter, and width are all braking considerations. The only downside to larger rotors is that stock wheels won't allow for the extra space. Tires and wheels are an area where it pays to plan ahead and get the size that is correct for the desired application and braking requirements. This is the starting point for any chassis build because this is the one thing you can't make or easily have custom made. Some companies offer low-profile calipers so you can run the largest rotor behind a smaller wheel, which is one option for enthusiasts looking to upgrade their brake system and still use factory-style wheels.

Modern mounting brackets from aftermarket manufacturers made it possible to mount larger floating calipers on stock-style spindles to improve the braking potential. The relocation of the caliper's mounting holes by the intermediate bracket are clearly visible here.

Fixed calipers have pistons on both sides of the caliper and are solidly mounted to the spindle. Fixed calipers need to be shimmed to fit the rotor properly.

Floating or sliding calipers are usually the two-pin design like the factory GM-style caliper in this photo. These calipers are easy to maintain and it is easy to change the brake pads, making them a popular choice for street vehicles.

Floating calipers, such as this one produced by CPP, have proven themselves as very safe daily driver choices. Manufacturing processes have changed and these units are very well built with greater technology than the original 1960s units. There are even color options that were not even an afterthought in the muscle car era.

Caliper Types

It is generally accepted that there are two basic types of brake calipers. The first is often referred to as the floating or sliding caliper. Floating calipers attach to a solidly mounted caliper bracket. The caliper itself is not solidly mounted and is allowed to slide left and right on pins and bushings that are mounted on the bracket.

When the driver steps on the brake pedal, the piston on the inner side of the caliper is actuated by the hydraulic pressure and pushes the brake pad out to the rotor. Because the rotor is solidly mounted and can't move side to side, the caliper is forced to slide until the brake pad from the other side contacts the rotors. The clamping force of

Fixed calipers are really only required when a vehicle has a large amount of speed or in a heavy vehicle with a moderate amount of speed when more powerful braking is needed.

The modern aftermarket mounting brackets have opened the door to more caliper options on front and rear brake systems. These brackets are made of billet material and are stronger than the surfaces they mount to in many cases. These brackets locate the caliper in the exact spot that provides the maximum braking potential.

the two brake pads slows down the rotating disc (rotor).

Because there are fewer parts in a floating caliper assembly, it is usually compact, lighter, and less expensive to make or purchase. These are major advantages of the floating brake caliper. Maintenance is simple and brake pads can be changed quickly and easily.

The second type of automotive brake caliper is a fixed caliper. Unlike the floating caliper, the entire caliper is solidly mounted in the fixed caliper system. Each side of the caliper has one or more pistons that push the brake pads to the rotor. Fixed calipers normally use multiple pistons with the same number of pistons on both sides of the caliper. These are usually configured in two pistons (one on each side), four pistons (two on each side), or six pistons (three on each side).

The most significant advantage of the fixed caliper system stems from the amount of clamping power that can be applied evenly to both sides of the rotor. Because the clamping force is applied evenly, fixed calipers are

said to provide better feedback and feel back to the driver through the brake pedal. This has made the fixed caliper brakes popular in modern luxury and performance cars. These have become a popular conversion or upgrade for cars from all eras.

In complete fairness to both styles of calipers, a floating caliper can offer much of the same performance of a fixed caliper at a lower price for many applications that are not high performance. The real difference shows up in high-performance and race conditions. The trade-off for this higher performance is cost and more frequent pad replacement and maintenance.

Deciding Which Caliper Type to Use

Both types of disc brake calipers are merited and can be used to make an effective braking system for autos from the muscle car era. The lightweight and inexpensive cost of floating caliper brakes makes them popular among many car enthusiasts. Muscle cars used as daily drivers are often treated to a floating caliper disc brake conversion from the stock drum brakes. These conversions are

efficient and work well even among modern compact cars in heavy traffic.

Highways full of lighter vehicles with modern braking technology pose a safety concern for heavier, mid-1960s muscle cars with drum brakes. At bare minimum, an entry-level floating caliper upgrade should be considered.

If the vehicle to be upgraded is built for speed or is a heavier vehicle with decent amounts of speed, a

Factory-style disc brakes from the muscle car era are generally larger cast-iron, single-piston calipers, such as the one pictured here. In addition to being easy to maintain, they are inexpensive to manufacture and cost less. This helped keep the cost of vehicles lower. The rotor in this photo is obviously an aftermarket upgrade.

The two-bolt caliper mounting for most auto manufacturers has been very similar for decades. This has given the aftermarket brake manufacturers the option to create mounting brackets that adapt newer calipers to the older spindles. The common two-bolt mounting system is clearly seen on the spindle in this photo.

Caliper size and number of pistons are tied together. The more pistons in the caliper, the larger the caliper housing needs to be. Brake companies work hard to keep the weight down so the caliper is designed to be no larger than it needs to be to work safely for a long time.

higher-performance braking system is required. Low-cost systems probably won't have the clamping force needed to stop these types of cars safely. A fixed caliper would be a great choice for this application.

Some vehicles are built with a proper balance of weight and speed that can handle fixed calipers on the front wheels and floating calipers on the rear wheels. Some brake manufacturers will provide a kit with this combination if they have tested the components with certain platforms.

High-Performance Caliper Considerations

Research is the key to getting the right system for your vehicle. Fortunately for us, muscle cars from the vintage muscle car era experienced few changes in design. That is to say, whole families of cars had very little change over generations.

For example, the two-bolt mounting for brake master cylinders on Fords and Chevy intermediate and full-size cars have been the same for decades. As a result, there is a large supply of components that fit a great number of different platforms. This applies to calipers as well.

Piston Size and Number: Larger and more pistons in the caliper increase

Size and placement matter when it comes to caliper pistons. Larger pistons placed at the rear edge of a brake caliper help prevent brake fade. Calipers with different-sized pistons are referred to as differential bore calipers.

the clamping power to the rotor. Pistons can range from 2 to 12 in higher-performance calipers.

Differential Bore Calipers: Engineers have discovered that it helps if the pistons closer to the rear edge of the caliper are larger in multi-piston calipers to increase the clamping force of the pistons and prevent brake fade. Differential bore calipers use a configuration with smaller pistons up front and larger pistons toward the back to achieve this improved clamping power.

Brake Rotor Choices

As we already discussed, the brake rotor or disc is where the kinetic energy to thermal energy conversion takes place. Most brake

discs are manufactured from a form of cast iron called "gray iron." This type of cast iron has a gray color due to the presence of graphite in the compound. It is also the most common type of cast-iron material, used in everything from internal-combustion engine cylinder blocks, to pump housings and valve bodies.

Gray iron has high thermal conductivity and a specific heat capacity that is perfect to make cast disc brake rotors. The Society of Automotive Engineers, now known as SAE International, sets standards for the manufacturing of gray iron. These specifications include the hardness, chemical composition, tensile strength, and other properties for automotive applications.

Almost every aftermarket brake manufacturer has entry-level and performance-level kits. These assembled kits contain the main components for a brake upgrade. In the case of the kit pictured above, this Master Power Brake kit was an upgrade from drums to disc brakes.

From stock OEM rotors to many high-performance types, these gray iron pieces are similar, but design plays a huge part in their usage. Some rotors are solid units; others are made with ventilation chambers (most often created during the casting process) running through the disc. These ventilation chambers act to dissipate heat and provide cooling. The size and amount of these ventilation chambers are evaluated for the size, weight, and power of the vehicle, as well as the purpose.

Brake discs often have holes or slots cut through the disc for better heat dissipation, to aid in surface-water dispersal, reduce noise and mass, eliminate outgassing created by the brake pads, and sometimes just for marketing cosmetics.

One thing that most experts agreed on is that there is no such thing as too much brake when it comes to the rotor and calipers. However, there is such a thing as too much brake pressure. Brake disc rotors must be broken in properly to get the best performance and wear correctly.

We cover a general break-in procedure in chapter 7. Most manufacturers refer to this as "bedding in" the rotor or pads. The procedure must be done before using the rotor and includes a thorough cleaning of the

Many rotors have slots, holes, or both cut into the rotor surface for various purposes. Recently, these holes have come into question on high-performance race applications. The stresses of racing can cause stress cracks in the rotor, usually originating at these holes. For non-racing applications, these holes probably pose no risk at all.

rotor to remove any preservation or machining oils.

If the manufacturer has included instructions for bedding in the rotors, follow their instructions. This physical bedding-in will include some moderate to heavy stops followed by a cooling period. This should be repeated several times until the rotor has been tempered to prevent thermal shock, distortion, or the formation of hot spots. Don't skip this step; it is worth the effort.

Application Selection

In basic terms, a brake system is unsprung weight that interferes with

a car's movement. The higher the unsprung weight, the lower the acceleration and top speed. Lighter components can help lower the unsprung weight and therefore help with acceleration, but in many cases, the cost can outweigh the benefits.

The two-piece rotor is the top choice of racers because of its better heat control and weight savings. These advantages are realized in two main ways with the first being the design.

The one-piece rotor is cast with the hat and the rotor in one unit. The two-piece rotor has a separate hat bolted to the rotor. The hat in a two-piece rotor is almost

Once rotors and pads are installed, they must be worn-in together to ensure safe and long use. Most manufacturers refer to this break-in as "bedding-in" of the rotor and brake pads. This rotor is a coated rotor that has not been through the bedding-in process. Rotors will typically have some marks from the process, even if they have a coating applied to the surface.

A two-piece rotor consists of a rotor and a separate rotor hat that is held together by bolts, snap rings, or other means. When the rotor is used beyond serviceable limits, only the rotor needs to be replaced. Over the long term, a two-piece rotor can be more economical. (Photo Courtesy Wilwood Engineering Inc.)

A one-piece rotor is cast by the manufacturer with the rotor hat and the rotor integrated into one unit. This is cost effective to make, but when the rotor is used up, the entire unit must be replaced.

always made of aluminum, which is lightweight and transfers heat well. This acts as a buffer to keep heat from the brake friction surfaces away from the bearings. The aluminum hat also allows the rotor to expand uniformly with distorting. This minimizes the chances of warpage.

Because the aluminum hat is bolted to the rotor, whenever the rotor is worn, only the rotor portion of a two-piece rotor needs to be replaced. There is a decent cost savings in that replacement alone. Initially the two-piece rotor is more expensive, and off-the-shelf parts at your local retail store aren't always available. Despite this, the two-piece

Making Brake Lines

Brake lines on 40-year-old cars often need replacing, and there's probably no better time to replace brake lines than during a brake system upgrade. If you've taken on the chore of swapping drum brakes to disc brakes, chances are that you are a do-it-yourselfer, and saving a few bucks by making your own brake lines sounds appealing.

Most aftermarket brake kits will specify which diameter size tubing should be used to support your new system. The two common brake line diameter sizes are 3/16-inch and 1/4-inch. Buy enough tubing and line nuts to complete the job. Bulk tubing in 25-foot rolls is available from most of the online parts stores, including Jegs and Summit Racing.

Brake line ends are double flared, which means the flare is folded over to create a double flare. This is far more secure than a single flare. A single flare is not able to handle the hydraulic pressure of an automotive brake system.

Special flaring tools are needed to create a double flare. An inexpensive flaring kit can be purchased at your local parts store for about $30. A leverage-style flaring tool can be pur-chased at specialty parts stores and manufacturers, such as Eastwood Auto Supplies. These do a great job but cost $200 or more. Unless you plan on doing a lot of brake lines, the inexpensive kit will take longer but get the job done.

Measure the new tubing to fit the line that will be replaced. Cut the line to size by using a tubing cutter. Most tubing cutters have an awl incorporated into the cutter. This awl is used to remove any burrs from the inside of the cut tube.

Put the brake tubing into the flaring tool and tighten the two sides down so the tube won't move. It helps to place the flaring tool in a bench vise to keep it secure. Read the instructions with the flaring tool to find out how much of the tube needs to stick out of the flaring tool. Do not overtighten the handle, otherwise the flare will split and become damaged.

Remove the die and repeat the flaring procedure to make the second part of the flare. This completes the double flair; the flaring tool can then be removed and the line placed in service. ∎

Making Brake Lines *Continued*

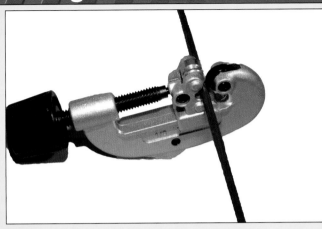

1   Start by measuring the tube and cutting it to length with a tubing cutter. These inexpensive cutters work with two hard steel cutting wheels that are tightened against the tubing. The entire cutter is rotated around the tubing, cutting a small line in the tube until it separates.

3   After the tube is cut and dressed, slide the appropriate-size line nut over the tube. Forgetting to slide the line nut on will make the tube useless and you will have to create another line.

5   After the first flare is made, remove the die and repeat the procedure to make the second flare. This 45-degree double flare is needed for automotive hydraulic brake systems.

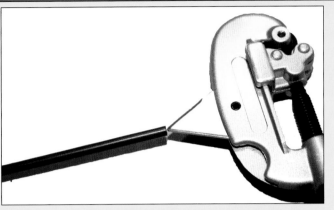

2   Most tubing cutters have a tool for removing burrs from the tube once it is cut. A small flat file can also be used to bevel and clean up the outside diameter of the cut tube.

4   Insert the double flare die inside the tubing, then clamp the line into the flaring tool. Tighten the flaring tool so the tube doesn't slip during the flaring process. It helps to put the flaring tool into a bench vise for more support.

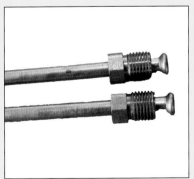

6   A properly double-flared tube will look like its flare is bubbled. These are often called bubble flares because of that look.

rotor is considered the best option for a serious racing setup.

Street Performance

As discussed, sometimes a simple move to single-piston, floating caliper disc brakes from drum brakes is all that is needed. For cars that will be used for lower-speed driving or daily commuting, these systems work well and replacement parts or consumables are available off the shelf at a parts store. This is an excellent economical choice as well.

Cars that will see higher-performance street/strip action or enter local car shows may want to move into an entry-level, powder coated, fixed caliper system with two pistons and drilled rotors, but consumables such as brake pads and rotors may not be as easy to get as OEM-style components.

Oval Tracks

The discs on a NASCAR short track car can reach temperatures as high as 1,800°F. Because of these amazingly high temperatures, these

Circle track brakes range from a factory-style GM floating brake to a wide-five hub-style braking system, such as the one shown here. These systems are used when wheel size is not a huge consideration but braking power is.

cars tend to use discs with extra-large ventilation channels to help dissipate heat faster. These ventilation channels are smaller on intermediate tracks and even smaller on super speedways. Understanding which type of track(s) your vehicle will be competing on is critical to brake selection.

The shorter the track, the more the brakes are used. In NASCAR's short tracks, such as Martinsville Speedway or Bristol Motor Speedway, the brake pedal is used more than the accelerator. Brakes are not only used to slow the cars down on short tracks but also to help these cars turn in the corner. On average, drivers will use the brakes up to 7 seconds in each set of corners. Lap times range from 19 seconds or more.

Road Races

Road racing requires higher braking force for each braking operation. Even with max deceleration, the temperatures remain cooler because longer straights allow the brakes to cool. In most well-designed road courses, drivers are only using the brakes about 30 percent of the total time on the track.

Street performance brake systems have become popular with 11- or 12-inch rotors with compact but powerful fixed calipers. This arrangement allows for the use of factory-style 15-inch steel wheels.

Road racing brakes are designed to manage heat and resist brake fade with heavy use. Road racers and autocross drivers favor wheels and brake systems that look as good as they perform.

Drag Strip

Like the other forms of racing, drag racing requires something a little more powerful and lighter than OEM stock brakes. Even in the entry-level or stock classes, the factory brakes on most vehicles are not up to the rapid deceleration needed at many tracks with short runoff room. Only in the mildest forms of drag racing will the stock brakes be adequate. Weight, material, and cooling channels are all design elements that should be considered when choosing the right brake system for any type of racing.

Drivers seeking competition typically move from the OEM single-piston caliper to a bolt-on two-piston caliper for street/strip applications. These calipers tend to have forged billet aluminum bodies, stainless steel pistons, and competition-style, high-temperature seals to handle faster speeds and daily commutes as well. As the racer progresses and speed improves, the next logical move is a kit with larger rotors and multi-piston calipers. This may even step into the four-piston caliper range.

Serious drag racers who rarely take their cars on the public roads will likely opt for a more specialized brake kit. These usually include direct-mount, lightweight steel rotors with aluminum hubs for weight considerations. Two- or four-piston forged-aluminum calipers and brake pads that handle higher temperatures are generally used.

Cars that are track-only race cars will move into a brake kit that has static holding power for staging and to supplement a parachute for stopping. These systems consist of a floating caliper with two or four

Drag racing brakes come in almost as many different styles as there are racing classes. Most feature hubs that allow for larger lug studs and a wider bolt circle. The mid-range level brake kit shown here is for a street/strip vehicle with calipers that can be mounted on the left or right side. Bleed screws on the top and bottom of the caliper allow for universal mounting.

pistons, solid steel rotors that may be drilled or undrilled, and an aluminum rotor hat and hub. Mount brackets will be billet aluminum, and all of the parts will be designed for strength and less weight.

Power or Manual Brakes

One of the first choices to be made in a brake upgrade is whether a manual brake system or power-assisted brake system is better for a project vehicle. Both types of brake systems only influence how the brakes are applied and not the actual clamping force of the brakes.

Many project car builders automatically choose power brakes, most with the misconception that power brake systems are better. The reality is that brake systems react the same no matter what supply side they have: power assist or manual.

The differences between manual and power-assist brakes are simply the physical effort at the pedal and pedal feel. Systems with power assist require less pedal effort by the operator to get to the same braking point as the manual system. Power-assist

The power-assist unit is a vacuum servo that uses vacuum to multiply the driver's pedal effort, then it applies that effort to the master cylinder. The vacuum booster is attached between the master cylinder and the brake pedal to assist the braking force applied by the driver. As shown here, vacuum boosters are offered in different sizes and colors depending on the manufacturer and the application.

systems can have slightly faster application due to the reduced pedal effort, but the difference in speed is not detectable from the driver's seat.

Baer Brakes' Bill Fowler recommends power-assist brakes for many car owners making the upgrade.

"If the engine in the car makes appropriate vacuum, and we suggest a minimum of 14 inches of vacuum at idle in gear with an automatic transmission, then a factory-style, vacuum-boosted system will be hard to beat. As an engine gets more radical and vacuum falls or boost is added, then the switch to a manual setup is a good idea."

Simply opting for a manual brake system by eliminating the power booster for economic reasons is possible but not the safest approach. It takes about 450 pounds of pressure to lock up the OEM brake drums on vintage muscle cars at speed. Disc brakes require almost double that, about 900 pounds of pressure for disc brakes to operate efficiently. That much pressure is easier to produce with a booster than just using leg power alone.

Creating Braking Force with Calipers and Master Cylinders

The Braking Force Production table shows the actual output force of different-size calipers resulting from 100 pounds of force input at the brake master cylinder. A $2^1/_2$-inch caliper actually puts out more braking force with a 3/4-inch master cylinder than a $2^{15}/_{16}$-inch caliper does with a 1-inch master cylinder, and nearly as much as a $2^{15}/_{16}$-inch caliper driven by a 7/8-inch master cylinder. It is actually possible to *increase* braking force using smaller calipers.

Research

The most important aspect of brake selection is research. Making yourself thoroughly knowledgeable in your type of motorsport is crucial. Knowing which brake pad material for your application will help in the safety department.

In addition to knowing the demands of the motorsport, an in-depth knowledge of your vehicle's traits is needed. Engineers in the 1960s had no idea these cars would last 40 years, and ultimately, they had no idea how far technology would advance in that time frame.

Master Power Brakes' Mark Chichester explained the engineering of brake systems during the muscle car heyday. "In that era, they didn't know what they didn't know," he said. "Some of the ways that calipers were retained on spindles was just crazy and very inefficient. Today nobody would even consider building systems that way."

Each application should be researched, and researched for the type of driving that the vehicle will be participating in. For example, a daily driver may have a rotor disc that is covered with a coating. Many manufacturers coat the cast-iron disc with a zinc coating. These look great and do a fine job of stopping at highway speeds and city driving.

While there was some strange factory caliper mountings in the 1960s, the Big Three manufacturers used pretty reliable spindle mounting for their cast calipers. This photo shows a typical GM caliper mounting on a 1972 Chevy Nova. This same type of mounting exists today.

Under high-performance applications, a zinc-coated rotor can warp with severe usage. This happens when the coating melts and gets redeposited unevenly on the rotor. Your brake pads can also become saturated with these zinc deposits and lessen their ability to work properly.

According to Fowler, brake pads have made the biggest gains in technology of all the components in the brake system. During their introduction in the muscle car era, brake pads generated a lot of outgassing during heavy use. These gasses would interfere with brake pad-to-rotor contact. With the selection of modern brake pads on the market these days, outgassing is no longer a problem when the correct pads are used for the application.

Before pad materials all but eliminated outgassing, brake companies offered disc rotors with holes drilled in them to help with the off-gassing. These cross-drilled holes became a sign of a quality brake rotor, so customers continued to request these

Braking Force Production		
Caliper	Master Cylinder	Braking Force (pounds)
$2^{15}/_{16}$ inches (6.777 square inches)	3/4 inch	1,536.372
	7/8 inch	1,127.734
	1 inch	863.308
$2^3/_4$ inches (5.939 square inches)	3/4 inch	1,346.710
	7/8 inch	988.184
	1 inch	756.557
$2^1/_2$ inches (4.908 square inches)	3/4 inch	1,112.923
	7/8 inch	816.637
	1 inch	625.220

No components in the brake system have changed as much over the decades as the brake pads. From leather to asbestos, organic, carbon, Kevlar, and ceramic materials, brake pads have changed dramatically. Along with the material changes, the brake pad outgassing properties have changed. This has led to changes in disc brake rotor designs. (Photo Courtesy Wilwood Engineering Inc.)

Manufacturers offer brake kits with various options; some have extra hardware and shims to help locate the caliper correctly on the rotor, such as this kit from Wilwood. (Photo Courtesy Wilwood Engineering Inc.)

rotors. Unfortunately, these holes have been found to cause stress cracks to form.

Baer Brakes became well known for its cross-drilled and slotted rotors. Ironically, Fowler says that Baer no longer recommends cross-drilled rotors for high-performance racing braking systems because of the potential for stress cracks.

Most aftermarket brake manufacturers offer different lines of brake kits assembled for specific applications. Baer Brakes has kits for just about every motorsport and automotive application. (Photo Courtesy Baer Brakes)

The Final Selection

Keeping in mind that new products and kits are continuously being developed and introduced to the market, the main word in brake system is *system*. It is possible to source all the components from various manufacturers and end up with a fully functioning, balanced brake system, but it will be a time-consuming process the odds of which are not with you.

Master Power Brakes' Chichester has witnessed this numerous times. "Some people will buy their front wheel components from one supplier, then buy the supply system from another. We see a lot of wrong bore sizes in the master cylinder when that happens. This makes the pedal feel totally unlike what it should. The best advice for anyone is to purchase products or a system from one vendor."

On that note, almost every brake professional in the aftermarket automotive world would agree that any customer will get the best results if he or she works with a company that helps them get a complete package for their needs.

Almost everyone is working on a budget, but some budgets are larger than others. If you have selected a kit or designed a system that fits your needs but find out that an additional part would help you get to your goal, wait for it. Additional parts, such as purpose-built tubular control arms, an adjustable proportioning valve, or a new master cylinder, could add to the cost and break your budget. It is advisable to wait until you have everything you want in a braking system before you attempt to make a system swap. This method will prove to be effective in braking power, the cost of parts, and your time.

GM BRAKE CONVERSION: BUDGET-FRIENDLY UPGRADE

Chevelles and their A-Body cousins were the rowdy kids of the late 1960s and early 1970s. Performance was all about going fast in a straight line. Chevelle, GTO, GS Buick, Tempest, LeMans, and 442 cars did that very well. Braking performance wasn't completely overlooked, but it certainly was not given all the attention it deserved. After all, speed was about going fast, not stopping fast.

It wasn't until the adolescence of the muscle car when the first front disc brake option finally became available. However, with the main focus on big-blocks, transmissions, and gearing, disc brakes remained a rare option and perhaps were even thought of more for the fledgling road-racing series than as a serious component for the strip and boulevard bully.

In this chapter, our focus is on a budget-friendly installation of a four-wheel disc brake upgrade on a first-year Chevelle. The test car is a manual-brake, single-reservoir master cylinder car that was fit (similar to all Malibus of the first few years) with drum brakes on each corner. Stock

GM midsize cars have become very popular with the muscle car crowd. The powerful Chevelle tops the list for many enthusiasts. These models can be found at the drag strip, on the road course, on the surface streets in Everytown, USA, and at the autocross course.

One way to do a budget upgrade is to use modern calipers from different models to take advantage of technology without spending a lot of money. This 1969 Camaro was fitted with a set of Z06 C6 Corvette calipers.

Classic Performance Products (CCP) offers brake upgrades and complete kits for a number of Chevrolet models and applications. The kit we installed was supplied with new rotors, spindles, single-piston calipers, brake hoses and rear lines, brackets, the master cylinder, and booster. Most of the CPP kits for these GM A-Body cars include a choice of booster size from 7, 8, 9, or 11 inches. Drop spindles are an option for those wanting to lower the stance and center of gravity but still maintain full suspension travel. The overall result is improved ride and handling characteristics. Slotted and drilled rotors can also be had for an extra cost. These kits are about as complete as they come.

The single-piston, floating caliper technology that General Motors rolled out in the early 1970s is still alive and well in aftermarket brake kits on the market today. This technology is still appropriate for daily driver street cars currently on the roads.

wheels were standard Kelsey-Hayes welded steel 14x5-inch models with a 1-inch offset.

This upgrade consists of a complete kit from Classic Performance Products (CPP) along with the addition of power assist via a vacuum booster. CPP went through a lot of work to assemble all of the required components so an average do-it-yourselfer would be able to complete the installation with basic hand tools and maybe a little help from a buddy over a weekend.

The kit is based on single-piston calipers that were used on thousands of vehicles from the late 1980s. We will cover these calipers in greater detail under the disc and caliper sections. For now, it will suffice to explain that these calipers work in conjunction with 10-inch rotors that fit most 15-inch wheels.

Wheel fitment is a vital consideration when you're upgrading the brakes on your muscle car. Remember, many of these cars from the muscle car era were fitted with 14-inch wheels from the factory, so wheel clearance is one of the critical aspects to check prior to choosing a brake upgrade kit.

Our upgrade was done on a Malibu with stock-type wheels, but most of these OEM-style front disc brake upgrades will work well with any 15-inch or larger wheel. Here is an example of a single-piston, GM-style caliper with an aftermarket wheel.

Beat the Drums

Drum brakes have their place but are better suited to the more pedestrian cars of the day, such as a four-banger Chevy II. When you could order a 375-hp 396-ci 4-speed Chevelle with 4.10:1 gears direct from the factory, those spindly 9.5-inch drums were severely outmatched. When brand new, the drums worked well for the average driver. As those enthusiasts lucky enough to have lived through that era will attest, the cars did brake acceptably well considering the rather rock-hard tires of the day.

The question wasn't if these cars would stop in a decent distance. The better question was whether they could muster the effort more than once. Freeway antics in today's world can easily create a situation where a panic stop from 70 mph to a standstill is quickly followed by acceleration back up to 70 mph that almost immediately calls for another dramatic slowdown. If insufficient time has passed to allow the brakes to cool, that second effort might call for some evasive maneuvers in a Chevelle with front drum brakes.

For purists who feel the need to retain those drum binders, there are not many brake shoe options available as upgrades. The early Chevelles and their A-Body cousins used a 9.5-inch drum set in the front with a 2.5-inch-width brake shoe, while the rears were the same diameter but narrower at just 2 inches.

Certain applications of A-Bodies, especially with El Caminos, have 11-inch drums on the rear to improve braking due to higher anticipated bed loads. Of course, these demand their own set of shoes because the smaller 9.5-inch drums and shoes will not interchange.

The secondary (trailing) brake shoe on the left is much longer than the primary brake shoe on the right. The secondary brake shoe provides more of the braking force.

Drum Brake Shoes

A set of four drum brake shoes will come in the box and the first thing any installer must do is separate the shoes into primary and secondary versions. If you look closely at the shoes, you will notice that the secondary shoe uses a slightly longer length of brake material than its primary partner. The primary shoe always is installed as the leading shoe: facing forward. The secondary shoe is always located on the trailing or rear position.

The reason for this shoe placement is what the industry referred to as the self-energizing (servo) action of most drum brake systems. When the wheel cylinder is activated, the pistons push both the primary and secondary shoes outward.

Looking at the drum system for the left front for example, the primary shoe hits the rotating drum and is immediately forced into a counterclockwise motion. The adjustable link bar at the bottom of the shoe attaches to the secondary shoe and forces the larger secondary shoe into the drum with more force. This is why the secondary shoe is fitted with more friction surface area.

A common issue that crops up with drum brakes is when the installer fails to realize the shoes are different, ending up with a pair of primaries on one side of the car and a pair of larger secondary shoes on the opposite side. When installed in this incorrect fashion, the car will pull hard to the side with the secondary shoes whenever the brakes are applied. Of course, the best way to avoid this is to install the shoes correctly.

Backing Plates

While we're on the subject of improving drum brake efficiency, high-mileage cars often suffer from grooved backing plates where the shoe slides across the backing plate during braking. These grooves restrict movement of the shoes, which reduces their effectiveness.

There are backing plates reproduced by Right Stuff Detailing, so replacement parts are available, but you can also repair original plates by merely MIG welding material into the grooves and then smoothing the weld back to a level surface. It's a cheap repair and not difficult if you have access to a MIG welder.

If the plan is to rebuild a drum brake set, just consider replacing everything, including the drum. Complete rebuild kits with all the springs and small parts are still available through companies such as Raybestos or Wagner, and these usually include the wheel cylinders.

If the car has been sitting and the wheel cylinders are corroded, don't try to rebuild the cylinders since they will just leak past the pitting in the cylinder. A small dab of white lithium grease on all brake shoe contact points will help the shoes slide across the backing plates.

Discs

We won't spend much time on the two-year-only 1967–1968 Chevelle front disc brake setup. This system resembles the early Corvette and 1967 Camaro disc brakes that used a fixed four-piston caliper. While this system worked reasonably well, it suffers from a significant design flaw.

The flaw is that hydraulic pistons use rubber seals located on the pistons, sealing to the cast-iron caliper cylinders. These calipers were bolted over 11-inch rotors. After a few years with brake fluid absorbing water like it is prone to do, these four-piston cylinders began to corrode, leaving rust spots that soon allowed brake fluid to leak past.

Later brake upgrades fixed the seal into the cylinder bore and sealed against the piston. The pistons generally are made of a harder material and don't corrode as easily, so the system is less susceptible to leakage. These calipers are still available but require a specific 1967 or 1968 A-Body spindle because this design was carried over in the 1968 model year with the new Chevelle body style. As with many of these calipers, they are specific to the right or left side because of the bleeder screw location. If the sides are inadvertently swapped, the bleeder screw will be on the bottom and of little use for bleeding the brakes.

It is possible to apply stainless steel sleeves to original factory cali-

General Motors switched to a single-piston, floating caliper in 1969. This caliper design became a staple for GM models for decades.

GM's single-piston, floating caliper used a mount that incorporated large metal pins that the calipers slid along. This design put most of the load on the inboard pad where the piston made contact.

pers when doing a restoration. The first company to offer this option commercially was Stainless Steel Brakes, but other companies now also perform this task. One company we discovered is called RK Sleeving in Upland, California.

Starting in 1969, General Motors converted to the now-familiar large single-piston, floating caliper that became the standard for decades. The single piston is located on the inboard side and uses a mount that allows the caliper to slide along large metal pins that pull the outboard brake pad into the rotor. As you can guess, there is a quite a bit of compliance in this design, which places most of the load on the inboard pad, so these tend to wear more quickly.

Even with this sliding caliper, the system is very robust and retained the 11-inch rotor diameter from the original 1967 four-piston calipers. While

many performance brake companies downplay this system, it includes the widely used GM D52-style brake pad. What's good about this popular brake pad is that just about every brake pad company in the world makes a pad for this application, so a lot of choices are available when it comes to pad selection.

Spindles, Reservoirs, and Boosters

This system was retained throughout the Chevelle era from 1969 through 1972 and makes an easy conversion for earlier A-Bodies. The spindles don't even need to be changed. Later spindles used larger bolts to attach the steering arm that will have to be drilled out with a hand drill or drill press. The disc brake floating calipers work well as long as the cast-iron slides do not become corroded and the large pins remain clean.

For early Chevelles and A-Bodies, this conversion will also demand dumping the original single-reservoir master cylinder and replacing it with a dual reservoir, which also requires some custom brake plumbing. A standard 1-inch nonpower master cylinder for a 1969 Chevelle will bolt in place of a standard nonpower early single-reservoir master cylinder, so that's a no-brainer, although we don't really like the high pedal effort.

Some enthusiasts think that disc brakes also require a power booster, but this is not entirely true. It's possible to use a nonpower master with front disc brakes and the only real cost is slightly higher pedal effort.

My experience with early Chevelles revealed that using a 7/8- or 15/16-inch-diameter piston master cylinder dramatically increases the line pressure to the front calipers and also to the back brakes. This reduces pedal effort but also increases pedal travel to make up for the lost volume using the smaller master cylinder piston.

To some people, this extra pedal travel can make the pedal feel mushy when in reality it is just additional travel necessary to move the fluid. While a small point, it is noticeable and some may find it objectionable. For everyone else, you become acclimated pretty quickly.

The physics behind this move is simple: a smaller master cylinder piston creates more pressure with the same amount of pedal effort. How much is this worth? We'll save you the math and just give you the numbers: With a typical 75-pound load applied to the brake pedal with a 6:1 pedal ratio, this applies 450 pounds of force on the master cylinder. A 1-inch master will generate 573 psi of brake line pressure, while a 7/8-inch master cylinder piston will bump that pressure up to 748 psi, a 30-percent increase in line pressure. You will notice that immediately.

Conversely, adding a larger $1^{1}/_{8}$-inch master using the same pedal forces as above will reduce the line pressure from 573 psi to 454 psi, which is a 20-percent reduction or drop in line pressure. That means you will have to step on the brake pedal 20-percent harder to apply the same braking force to the tires. This could easily set up a condition where it would be nearly impossible to lock the brakes with the larger master cylinder.

What all this means is: if you are considering changing master cylinder sizes, even a 1/16-inch change in piston diameter can have a drastic effect on braking performance.

Proportioning Valve

Of course, adding a front disc brake system to a drum brake car also requires some type of brake pressure proportioning system to reduce the higher hydraulic pressure to the rear brakes. If a proportioning valve is not employed, the high pressure will prematurely lock up the rear brakes under heavy braking.

Many inexpensive front disc brake conversion kits come with a factory-style combination valve that reduces the rear brake pressure. While this is certainly better than no valve at all, it does not and cannot account for the dozen or so variables that are integrated into your particular application. Let's look at an example.

The combination valve usually incorporates an isolation valve in the system. The isolation valve is controlled by the front and rear incoming brake pressure. This valve has incoming brake pressure acting on each side of a piston. If the pressure on one side of the piston is more than the other side, the piston will start moving toward the lower pressure. At a predetermined point of piston movement, the brake light warning switch is triggered.

Let's say that we want to convert a 1964 El Camino from four-wheel drums to factory single-piston caliper front brakes by using a complete spindle and brake assembly from a 1969 Chevelle. While both cars share the same wheelbase, the El Camino is significantly lighter in the rear with its bed, putting less weight over the rear tires.

In this particular application, this 1964 El Camino happens to be equipped with larger 11-inch rear

The size of the master cylinder piston has a direct effect on the amount of pressure created by the effort placed on the brake pedal. A smaller piston creates more pressure with the same pedal effort than a larger piston does. (Photo Courtesy Wilwood Engineering Inc.)

How to Adjust a Proportioning Valve

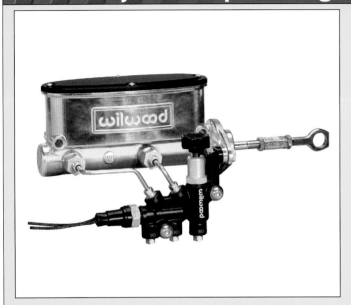

An adjustable brake proportioning valve allows the user to fine-tune the front-to-rear braking balance by proportionally decreasing the rear brake line pressure. The proportioning valve can be mounted in several different locations, including plumbed directly into the master cylinder. (Photo Courtesy Wilwood Engineering Inc.)

The best place to install a proportioning valve is between the line running to the rear brakes from the master cylinder. Often these valves are placed just below the master cylinder. Choose a place where it is convenient to access. I've even seen them placed inside the lower rocker panel where the driver can access it from the driver's seat by opening the door and reaching inside the frame.

The purpose of the proportioning valve is to reduce the pressure generated by the master to the rear brakes to compensate for the inevitable weight transfer that occurs under heavy braking. Older muscle cars such as Chevelles tend to exhibit severe nosedive under hard braking because half of the engine is located in front of the front-axle centerline.

This nosedive moves significant weight from the rear of the car to the front, reducing the weight over the rear tires. This reduction in load on the rear tires requires much less hydraulic brake pressure to prevent prematurely locking up the rear tires.

When rear brake lockup occurs, vehicle control with the rear tires is lost and the rear will tend to come around,

forcing the driver to modulate the brake pedal to reduce the pressure to unlock the rear brakes and regain control of the car. This reduces the overall brake efficiency and increases the stopping distance.

By custom tuning the rear brake pressure, the driver can apply maximum brake pressure right on the edge of impending tire lockup, which is where the car will stop in the least amount of time and distance.

Items such as the amount of fuel in the tank and tire pressure have a big impact on adjusting the brake proportioning valve, so set the tire pressures and test the car with a half tank of fuel as a good starting point. You will also need a long, wide, preferably multi-lane, straight road with no traffic in either direction in order to safely drive and test the car. It's best to start by setting the proportioning valve at its lowest pressure setting.

Start first by accelerating to roughly 40 mph and stopping aggressively without locking up the front brakes. If only the rear brakes lock up, do not do any more testing. You will need to reduce the caliper piston size on the rear brakes if they are discs. We've seen this happen with an early Camaro that was fitted with a Ford 9-inch rear end with large single-piston caliper rear discs that would lock up with the proportioning valve fully released. This occurs because the rear caliper pistons were too large. If you are considering a rear disc kit with very large pistons, do the math we outlined in this chapter to evaluate the pressures this system will create.

Assuming the rear brakes do not lock up early, move to 50 mph and repeat the test. If there is still no lockup, increase the rear pressure in one-turn increments until the rear brakes lock up before the fronts. Then return the proportioning valve to its best previous position. I have to emphasize that this must be accomplished in a safe and careful manner to prevent loss of vehicle control from brake lockup. Crashing your car while setting the brake prop valve is bad form; don't be that guy.

It's also best to back the rear brake pressure down from the most aggressive setting for street driving to accommodate differences in driving conditions as you may not always be driving on a nice clean road with concrete for traction. And again, if the rear brakes lockup up prematurely, always react by lifting slightly off the brake pedal to restore traction to the rear tires. Anytime the tires are sliding, control of the vehicle is lost. ∎

drums and taller 275/60R-15 rear tires mounted on 15x8-inch wheels with 5.5-inch rear backspacing. All of these are non-stock changes compared to a stock 1969 Chevelle combination valve and will drastically affect when the rear brakes lock up during emergency braking.

This really forces the issue to employ an adjustable proportioning valve for any front disc brake conversion. You've probably read a commonly used number that approximately 70 percent of braking effort comes from the front brakes under hard braking. Weight transfer from the rear of the vehicle to front makes braking force substantial on the front brakes.

Despite this common belief, my experience with high-performance brake systems on early GM A-Body muscle cars reveals that a very large percentage of braking efficiency comes from those tiny 9.5-inch rear drum brakes. It pays large dividends to apply as much braking energy to the rear brakes as possible.

Upgrades

Several upgrades can be performed to the 11-inch Chevelle rotor and floating caliper world that do not require thousands of dollars to achieve. A quality set of performance 11-inch rotors attenuated with a set of performance pads, such as those from Baer Brakes, EBC Brakes, Hawk Performance, Performance Friction Corporation (PFC), Raybestos, and many others, is a great place to start. Look for a pad that has good street characteristics, such as good cold friction and reliable initial feel with a clean release, one that is not noisy or exhibits excessive brake dust because that's just material you have to constantly clean off your wheels. There are several brake pad manufacturers that offer brake pads that fit this category, including EBC Brakes, Hawk Performance, PFC, and Raybestos.

Another simple upgrade is to replace the stock OEM rubber flexible lines with DOT-rated stainless steel hoses and fittings. These hoses do no deflect under pressure and will help deliver a more solid brake pedal feel. Several companies, such as Russell and Earl, offer affordable stainless steel hoses. Just the change to new brake fluid, hoses, and brake pads can make a dramatic change to braking performance while keeping the cost under just what a pair of 14-inch rotors would demand. Not everybody needs 14-inch four-wheel disc brakes with six-piston calipers.

Rotors

Huge brakes have become the signature components of the Pro Touring push since the turn of the 21st century. They look amazing inside a set of 18- or 20-inch wheels and those slots, holes, and dimples just add to the bling. But what's really going on here? Is all that really necessary?

Large rotor diameters do serve a useful purpose. Brakes are much like a clutch in a manual-transmission car. The larger clutch adds surface area which adds holding power. A larger rotor increases surface area (often called swept area), but more importantly, the diameter adds leverage. As diameter increases, this moves the caliper farther away from the spindle centerline, which gives the caliper more leverage over the kinetic energy of the moving vehicle.

Larger-diameter rotors also demand larger-diameter wheels to clear the caliper. These are not hard and fast rules, but a 12-inch factory rotor and caliper will *usually* fit inside a 15-inch wheel. A 13-inch rotor package will *sometimes*

Companies, such as Wilwood Engineering, offer several different brake pad lines. From the low- and mid-temperature/ friction lines for street use to full competition high temperature/friction use. (Photo Courtesy Wilwood Engineering Inc.)

Rotors with drilled holes are stylish and serve a purpose. Brake pads can outgas under heavy braking conditions. These drilled holes allow the brake gases to escape as the temperature rises.

fit inside certain 16-inch wheels and certainly 17-inch wheels. The 14-inch rotor packages will demand at least an 18-inch-diameter wheel, so keep these relationships in mind when choosing a brake rotor size. Bigger almost always means more expensive, often in more ways than one.

Drilled holes are often thought of as stylish, but they do serve a purpose. Under heavy braking, brake gases need a place to escape as the temperature spikes. Unfortunately, these drilled holes offer an excellent starting place for stress cracks that will eventually cause rotor failure. Rotor technology and materials help fight this, but a better idea is rotors equipped with dimples or slots cut into the rotor face. These depressions perform the same function as holes but do not offer the starting point for stress cranks, which improves the rotor's life expectancy. Most companies offer dimples and grooves as options for their performance rotors.

Cryogenics is another word that has crept into the high-performance lexicon. Some claim that this subzero exposure of the metals helps align iron crystals and improve the durability of the metallurgy, allowing the rotor to better withstand the heat of high braking temperatures. My research has led to no such results, and I have yet to find credible results that would lead to similar conclusions. While cryogenic freezing has its proponents, at this time many still remain skeptical. There may be better ways to spend your money.

Calipers

The main advantage of larger, multi-piston calipers is a combination of extending the swept contact area of a larger pad and adding pistons that can evenly apply the pad against the rotor. The main function of the caliper piston(s) is to generate clamp load. Brakes work by a combination of coefficient of friction of the pad applied with a given load over a given area positioned by the diameter of the rotor. Longer pads with more surface area require more pressure and multiple pistons make that happen.

Another advantage of multiple piston calipers is that the load applied is spread out over a larger area on the pad, leading to more even pad wear. This is one of the disadvantages of the original large, single-piston GM calipers. A recent innovation on multiple piston calipers is using a smaller piston on the pad's leading edge followed by larger pistons toward the trailing edge. This also contributes to more even pad wear since the leading edge of any pad tends to accelerate wear and it digs into the spinning rotor.

Most multiple-piston calipers are of the two-piece variety that are bolted together, often with a brake fluid transfer port that must be sealed. This two-piece construction makes the caliper easier to build. According to several brake industry experts, there are no real strength advantages to a mono-block or one-piece caliper design since the real test becomes the way the caliper is designed to resist the forces of pressure on both sides of the caliper, assuming a fixed-piston design that attempts to spread the caliper apart

The Contact Patch

After all of the discussion is over concerning brakes and braking power, the ultimate evaluation of good stopping distance is determined by the contact patch between the four tires and the road. To put this in perspective, the most killer full-carbon brake system that emulates all the best in brake technology will not be much help if the contact patch with the ground is limited either by four small tires or four tires that are past their prime and hard as a rock.

Even drum brakes have the ability to lock up all four tires in a panic stop. The point of maximum braking efficiency is having a brake system that will put a large amount of braking force through the tires and into the pavement. This requires the tires to do most of the work. If the tires are old, have lost compliancy, and are as hard as a plastic tabletop, they are not going to generate a high level of traction, and tons of braking energy will be lost because it cannot be transferred into the pavement.

Think of braking efficiency through the tires like straight-line acceleration. Tiny, rock hard tires are going to make putting 1,000 hp down to the track extremely difficult. Conversely, a huge pair of rear slicks will really be able to put that power down and accelerate the car. The same is true with brakes. A wide set of sticky front and rear tires will be able to plant a ton of braking force right into the pavement that will pull your 3,500-pound street car down from 60 mph in less than 110 feet and make it look easy. Just don't forget the tires are a big part of the package. ∎

Calipers with multi-pistons provide braking force that is evenly spread across the contact patch, resulting in more even pad wear. Almost every aftermarket brake manufacturer offers a multi-piston caliper as well as a single-piston caliper.

at the bridge where the caliper straddles the rotor. The bridge is any caliper's weakest point. So there does not appear to be any real strength advantage to a mono-block caliper.

Brake Pads

This is an area that becomes a strange mixture of chemical concoctions that is heavily influenced by heat, pressure, type of use, and personal preference. It might seem that it would be easy to create a brake pad material that could do everything well, but as with most things in life, there are compromises. For example, brake dust, noise, cold performance, life expectancy, pedal responsiveness, and a host of other details are all variables that affect the decision on a pad material.

A brake pad with a very high coefficient of friction will certainly improve stopping power and may perform well at very high temperatures but might destroy a set of rotors in less than 10,000 miles. This is not a good choice for a street car.

There are literally a dozen or so brake pad manufacturers, and it isn't possible to go into all the different configurations across all the major brands. If we were to break the pads down into categories, there are organic (non-asbestos) pads that are generally the direct-replacement pads, semimetallic pads, and ceramic material. The material differences generally follow increasingly higher temperature capacities for racing.

While some racing products can be used on the street, when it comes to disc brake pad material, these are best left for use on only road race or circle track applications. Higher-temperature pads as a general rule do not work well on street cars because it's rare for a street car to generate the elevated temperature necessary to make a race pad perform properly. Other areas of importance for street-driven cars are dust and noise, which are nonissues with race cars. So, leave the race pads for the race cars and you'll be better off.

Pedal Pulsation

One area that seems to garner a lot of attention is brake shudder or pedal pulsation. This is most often blamed on warped rotors. A white paper authored by noted race car builder Carroll Smith claims that rotors rarely warp and that the pedal pulsation is caused by a buildup of brake pad material on the face of the rotor that creates high spots that become extremely hard. These small peaks can be seen as hard blue spots on the rotor that cannot be removed by simple brake lathe cutting because these spots are incredibly hard. If the rotor is a two-piece design where the rotor can be separated from the hub, then the rotor can be Blanchard ground and the hot spots removed. Otherwise, the rotor must be replaced.

The best way to avoid the formation of these hot spots is to properly bed in new brake pads and/or new rotors. This bedding-in process creates sufficient heat to transfer pad material from the pad to the rotor. This demands a gradual application of significant heat, and often the process will be noticeable enough that you will smell the brakes as they cook off the bonding agents present in the pad material.

The important point when bedding in pads is to avoid coming to a complete stop after heating the pads. A full stop at high temperature can create an imprint of the pad on the rotor, which could easily create the high spots the bedding process intends to avoid. So, it's important that the specific brake pad manufacturer's bedding process recommendation is closely followed. To read more about this process, find the Carroll Smith white paper at StopTech.com.

Recommendations

It's difficult to make any kind of a street brake pad recommendation since there are so many different pad materials and compounds. Companies with a solid reputation for quality products include Baer Brakes, EBC Brakes, Hawk Performance, Performance Friction Corporation, Raybestos, StopTech, Wagner, Wilwood, and many others. If you are abusing your brakes under autocrossing or track day exercises, talk with some of the more-knowledgeable participants about their recommendations, especially if the pad will be used for both street and mild race use.

There are several brake pad manufacturers with equally as many different configurations in pad construction. Most are broken down into basic categories, such as organic and semi-metallic.

The most important point is to choose a pad that will withstand the heat it will be exposed to yet still generate decent cold-stop characteristics so that the brakes will work well the first time you step on the pedal. This is a characteristic that most race pads do not display, and it is the main reason that race pads should not be used on a street-driven car.

Rear Disc Upgrades

It's important to not overlook the contribution of rear brakes to overall braking performance. Many enthusiasts tend to focus on front brakes while often ignoring the rears. For the average street car, rear drum brakes are fine but if you do want to step up there are some interesting and relatively inexpensive upgrades for the Chevelle and A-Bodies that will not only offer improvements in braking power but also look good.

CPP offers several different versions of a single-piston floating caliper kit, one in particular is part number 1012RWBK-SE-6467 that includes a rear parking brake kit that is outlined in photos and captions with this chapter. There are several iterations of this kit available depending upon completeness.

Among the least expensive rear disc brake swaps are several kits that use parts from the third- and fourth-generation Camaro. Summit Racing (part number SUM-BK1623) and Right Stuff Detailing (part number AFXRD01) offer similar kits that supply the rotors, calipers, pads, mounting brackets, hoses, and even parking brake cables. These kits are competitively priced at under $400. If you want to do the job yourself using a combination of used/junkyard parts and new components, it's not very difficult.

The key component is the rear caliper mounting bracket that connects the rear axle housing to the caliper. The factory application uses two different brackets, but we've found that the large, heavy, cast-iron bracket works very well and bolts directly to the early 10- and 12-bolt A-Body rear axle assemblies. This will require removing the stock drum brake assembly, which means the hardest part of this whole conversion is removing the rear cover and pulling the C-clips to allow removing the rear axles. The new caliper brackets bolt in on the stock rear axle mounting flange. Slip the axle back in place, slide on the rotor and the caliper, and the main work is done. The only

thing left to do then is to install the metric flexible hose on each caliper. These use a short flexible hose because the caliper is free-floating. Adapt the metric fitting in the end of the hose to the hard line tee on the top of the rear axle.

This conversion is not in the least the only way to adapt rear disc brakes to a Chevelle. Baer Brakes, Wilwood, and many others also offer aftermarket kits in various rotor diameters and caliper configurations. If you desire to maintain 15-inch rear wheels to mount drag race slicks, keep in mind that larger rear rotor diameters will demand larger-diameter wheels. This can sometimes cause difficulties when you want to run predominantly drag race–style 15-inch rear tires. The third-generation 11.5-inch rear disc brake kit mentioned earlier is small enough to accommodate a 15-inch wheel.

This chapter really just begins to describe some of the various disc and drum brake options available to the enthusiast. Not everybody wants or needs a six-piston caliper brake system or even four-wheel disc brakes. It all comes down to what fits your budget and your sense of how much braking you need for how you plan to use the car. The rest of it is just fashion.

Budget Rear Disc Swap Parts List

We mentioned a budget process for rear disc brakes by using third-generation Camaro rear discs. If you buy the used calipers and mounting brackets at the junkyard, this can drastically reduce the cost of this conversion. This list includes both new rotor and rebuilt caliper part numbers and even the rear caliper mounting brackets.

We've found that RockAuto.com has some of the best prices and all these parts are available through that site. I've priced out new basic rotors, rebuilt calipers (including the cost of not having cores), along with a set of ceramic performance pads from Raybestos, and the cost of all the major parts came to less than $500. Of course, if you choose to buy the calipers and brackets used, the price plummets to less than $300.

The brake booster and proportioning valve in the front disc replacement kit are rated for the weight of the vehicle specified to ensure the correct front-to-rear pressure ratio. This prevents one set of axle brakes from stopping quicker than the other set. It is highly recommended by many professionals to install a separate 10-pound residual valve in the rear brake line to help keep sufficient pressure in the rear wheel cylinders.

This is a great way to add rear disc brakes while not spending a ton of money. ∎

Description	Part Number
Raybestos 11.6-inch rear rotor	6995
ACDelco 11.6-inch rear rotor	18A287
Raybestos ceramic rear brake pads	ATD413C
A1 Cardone rear caliper bracket (left and right)	141181
ACDelco rebuilt caliper (left rear)	18FR972
ACDelco rebuilt caliper (right rear)	18FR971
Wilwood adjustable proportioning valve	260-8419
Dorman flexible brake hose (left rear)	H380294
Dorman flexible brake hose (right rear)	H38612
Dorman metric banjo bolt (2)	484205

Rear Brake Install

The front brake assemblies come out of the box assembled with packed bearings and all. The loaded caliper and rotor still need to be removed for installation of the steering link bracket and to make it easier to mount to the ball joints on the car. The 11-inch vented rotors feature a stock-like solid surface that is 1.035 inches thick. Stock-style front spindles are included and come in various configurations that change the vehicle's stance. This particular kit came with stock-like spindles that retain the stock ride height.

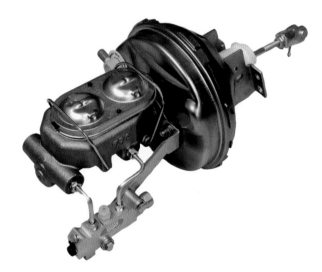

The Chevelle we are upgrading was equipped with manual brakes and it was definitely time to step up to a dual-reservoir master cylinder and power assist. The components are supplied fully assembled with the kit, including the combination valve to provide the correct brake bias. The combination valve is actually several valves in one. There is a brake light warning switch and isolation valve, a metering valve for the front brakes, and a proportioning valve for the rear brakes.

Removing Drum Hardware

1 The original rear drum brakes were still in fair shape, but the Chevelle was due for a serious braking upgrade. When planning for an upgrade, be sure to inspect the axle shafts for wear, as this would be the time to replace them, especially since you'll be installing new wheel studs. You should also check the lines that aren't being replaced for any cracking, leaking, or swollen and bulging lines. These are unsafe and should be replaced.

2 Cleanliness is very important. In order to keep the system clean and safe, make sure you clean the fittings and surrounding area before opening any part of the brake system. Before disassembling, spray the assembly off with brake cleaner, such as Driven Racing Oil's Brake & Parts Cleaner. This washes away a lot of the dust, dries quickly, and makes for an easier and cleaner disassembly process. Do not use compressed air to clean or dry brake components. Even filtered air may contain moisture or small traces of oil.

3 A brake shoe retaining spring tool isn't necessary to take apart drum brakes. However, they make things a lot easier, especially if you ever plan to maintain drum brakes. The brake spring removal tool also helps remove frustration by offering leverage to help remove drum brake washer springs. Start the removal by releasing the retaining springs on the front and rear pad then the parking brake spring and tensioners at the top.

4 Brake shoe retaining spring tools come in various designs, but the simplest and easiest to use has a handle like a screwdriver or nut driver. There is a range of sizes available from 5/8- to 7/8-inch cup ends on the brake shoe retaining spring tool. There are even models with a 5/8-inch cup on one end, a 7/8-inch cup on the opposite end, and a handle in the middle. For the cost, this is a simple tool that every mechanic should have in the toolbox, especially if working on cars with brake shoes.

Removing Drum Hardware *Continued*

5 Look at all the parts it takes to assemble a rear drum brake assembly. Drum brakes have a tendency to pull one way or the other during moderate to hard stopping. This pull varies as shoes wear, return springs fatigue from age, the pivot mechanisms wear, lubrication dries out, and any of the components seen here wear out. Not only is the clamping function of a disc caliper more effective, it is also easier to build and maintain.

Rear End Prep

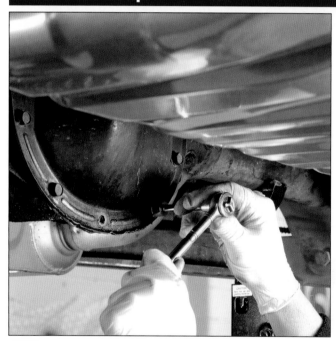

1 With the brake shoes and hardware stripped, it's time to pull the axles. On a Chevelle, you'll need remove the differential cover to access the C-clamps that retain the axles. There's no drain plug, so just remove the cover bolts from the bottom up and be ready with a large-diameter drain pan. The 10- and 12-bolt rear ends hold about 2 quarts. Most Chevelles manufactured from 1964 to 1972 were delivered from the factory with the GM 10-bolt rear end.

2 Locate and remove the small bolt (usually a 5/16-inch head) that goes through the center pin of the carrier. This is the pinion shaft lock bolt. The idea is to remove this bolt so the pinion shaft can be moved out of the way. When keeping the same rear end and not making any other changes, it is imperative to not remove the pinion shaft all the way out. As long as the pinion shaft is not completely removed, the setup of the rear end will not be altered. Note that you may need to rotate the driveshaft. Remove the bolt and push the pin out of the way, using care to keep the pinion shaft and spider gears in place. Many experienced mechanics place a piece of duct tape on the bottom of the carrier to ensure that the pinion shaft does not come all the way out after the bolt is removed.

Rear End Prep *Continued*

3 Push the axles inward to release the C-clip. If the C-clips can't be removed with your fingers, use a magnet or needle-nose pliers to grab the clips and remove them. Yes, this is all that holds the axles and the wheels in place on a Chevy. The design has worked well for millions of vehicles, but if you plan on making serious horsepower or competing on autocross tracks, a C-clip eliminator kit or a complete rear end aftermarket upgrade might be considered. The 12-bolt rear ends are getting harder to find in the wrecking yards, but several aftermarket choices are available. For our application, we're sticking with what we have.

4 With the C-clips removed, the axles slide easily out of the housing, allowing you to remove the four retainers that secure the backing plate. The parking brake cable can also be removed because the CPP kit is supplied with new cables. Remove the backing plates and parking brake cables. This is the last step before assembly, so take the time to clean up and organize your tools and parts.

5 CPP supplies two brackets that mount to the rear axle housing. These two brackets are heavy-duty steel pieces that are engineered to provide the proper spacing and serve as a secure mount for the new caliper. Mounting hardware and mount spacers are also supplied. The caliper and rotor tolerance is tight to improve friction contact between the pads and rotor.

6 The caliper mounts, along with the spacers provided by CPP, locate the caliper over the rotor precisely.

Rear End Prep *Continued*

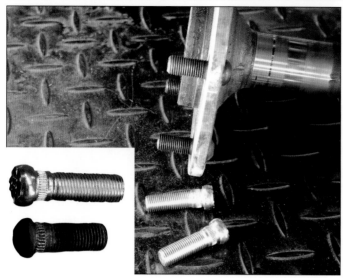

7 Longer wheel studs are required to compensate for the rotor flange thickness versus that of the stock thin drum flange. It may be tempting to use a big hammer and brass drift to remove and install the wheel studs, but if the factory axles are used, it's best to use a press or a large vise to properly remove the old studs and install the new ones. Using the lug nut to pull the stud into the flange should be avoided. Use caution to prevent damage to the stud's threads or the shoulder of the lug nuts.

8 Inspect the splines on the end of the axles as well as at the end where the bearing and seal ride. Chevelle rear wheel bearings use the axle as an inner race and the bearing rollers ride directly on the axle shaft itself. If you have worn or pitted rollers, if chipped or damaged bearings have worn a groove into the axle shaft, or if the seal has worn a groove into the axle shaft, it may be necessary to replace the axle shaft assembly, bearings, and seal. Even if the bearings are still serviceable, this is a prime time to replace the axle bearings.

9 It's also a best practice to replace the axle seals while you're at this point. Use a seal removal tool to prevent damaging the axle tube and tap the new seal into place. Place a little lube on the lip of the seal and carefully install the axle without dragging it over the new seal. Install the C-clips to secure the axles at this juncture.

Installing the New Brake Hardware

1 After reinstalling the axles, clean the rotor of machining oils with brake cleaner, then install the assembly.

2 Here is the new caliper. Note the parking brake assembly on top, which was inspected and prepped for installation. Make sure the pads are opened enough to easily clear the rotor. You may need to press the piston into the caliper to make room.

3 The caliper slipped right over the rotor and lined up with the mounting brackets. Long, hex-headed bolts are supplied to secure the caliper. Note that the caliper mounts have a flexible isolator and bushing. These must be in place to allow the caliper to move as the pads wear.

4 The rear installation is complete. It now has more effective and consistent braking with a lot fewer parts. With the calipers in place, it is time to button up the differential cover, connect the lines, and install the parking brake cables.

5 When routing the hard lines across the rear axle, secure them with clamps or by using the original locking tabs to keep the lines in place.

Installing the New Brake Hardware *Continued*

6 *Before installing the differential cover, we pulled off the factory brake line T from the original lines. CPP supplied two new hard lines and we opted to replace the rubber line that connects from the chassis hard line to the rear end. Note the bracket that secures the assembly to the rear end cover.*

7 *Once everything was assembled and lines were connected, the differential cover was cleaned and the new gasket was located (two were supplied with the kit). It is best to use a thin coat of gasket sealer to form an effective seal. Also, don't forget to fill up the differential with the proper lubricant.*

Install the Parking Brake Cable

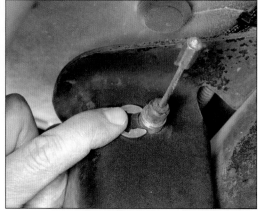

CPP supplies new parking brake cables. First, remove the original cables from the chassis and disconnect them from the main cable connector. The new cables mount in the factory locations on the chassis with a C-clip.

The cable can be installed with the caliper mounted, but to show the connection and retaining C-clip these photos were taken with the caliper off. It's a tight squeeze, but the C-clip can be maneuvered into place under the spring to secure the new cable to the caliper assembly.

Front Brake Install

Remove Drum Assembly

1 Get started on the front brakes by removing the hub assembly and brake shoes. In the case of the Chevelle and CPP kit, the entire spindle and steering are going to be replaced.

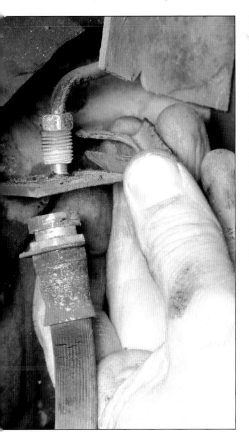  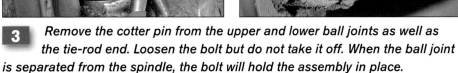

3 Remove the cotter pin from the upper and lower ball joints as well as the tie-rod end. Loosen the bolt but do not take it off. When the ball joint is separated from the spindle, the bolt will hold the assembly in place.

4 Before removing the spindle and brake assembly from the control arms, ensure that the lower control arm is secured to keep pressure on the coil spring using a floor jack. The weight of the car will help keep the spring slightly compressed. Use caution during disassembly: the coil spring is under load!

2 Disconnect the factory rubber hose from the retaining point on the chassis where they connect to a hard line. This hard line and location will be used with the new hose.

Front Disc Hardware Installation

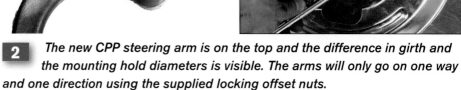

1 *Just like the rear, it is visible how much more efficient a modern disc brake setup is compared to a factory drum.*

2 *The new CPP steering arm is on the top and the difference in girth and the mounting hold diameters is visible. The arms will only go on one way and one direction using the supplied locking offset nuts.*

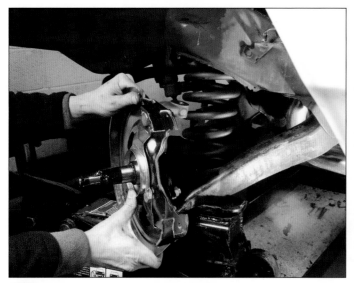

3 *With the new steering arms installed, the spindle assembly was positioned on the upper and lower ball joints (make sure the rubber boots are in good condition and in place). The castle nuts were reinstalled and torqued to 61 ft-lbs on the top and 83 ft-lbs on the bottom. New cotter pins were installed as well.*

4 *After ensuring that each bearing was packed full of grease, the spindle assembly was reinstalled. The bearing was pre-loaded and locked in place with a new cotter pin.*

5 Load the brake caliper with the brake pads and anti-rattle clips. The anti-rattle clips are always installed on the inner brake pad and, as the name implies, they help reduce brake noise by stopping the pad from rattling between the piston and the brake rotor.

6 The front caliper slid over the new rotor, and the long socket head cap screws were put into position and tightened.

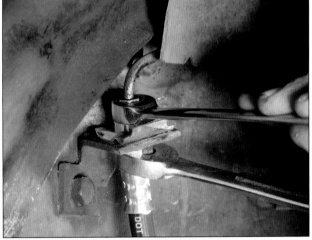

7 The new brake line was installed on the caliper, making sure to have the two compression washers in place and that the offset side of the mounting block was positioned correctly. The other end of the hose is connected to the hard line in the factory retainer.

8 Perform a safety check of your installation prior to bleeding the brake system. Never take anything for granted. Double-check each nut and bolt for security. Have an assistant turn the steering wheel from lock-to-lock and observe the lines and components for any interference. Check the passenger's side and the driver's side.

Master Cylinder and Booster Installation

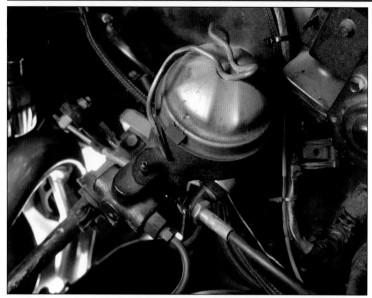

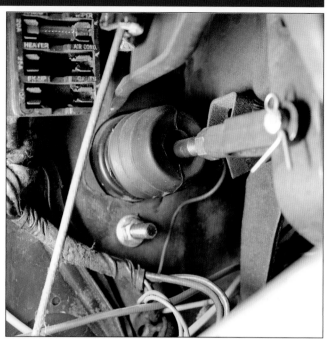

The factory single reservoir was one of the main reasons for upgrading the brake system. Plus, it was time to step up to power assist. Many muscle cars prior to 1968 used a single-reservoir brake master cylinder. This is not ideal or the safest brake system. If a master cylinder or one of the wheel's brake systems should fail, with only one brake line and reservoir, the entire brake system would fail. A dual-reservoir master cylinder keeps the front and rear braking systems completely separate from one another.

The master cylinder pushrod is held onto the brake pedal with a pivot pin secured with a cotter pin. Remove the cotter pin from the brake pedal to allow removal of the master cylinder from the car.

Loosen the brake lines at the master cylinder and remove the mounting bolts that hold the master cylinder to the firewall. The master cylinder can be removed from the vehicle, leaving the firewall bare and ready for the new master cylinder and brake booster combination.

This master cylinder, combination valve and brake booster were all assembled from CPP. The only lines left to connect are for the front and rear brakes. If the brake booster is a new addition and the old unit is not simply replaced, you may need to change the brake pedal if you have an automatic transmission. Cars with power brakes and automatic transmissions were equipped with a wider brake pedal.

Master Cylinder and Booster Installation *Continued*

The vacuum booster mounts to the firewall, directly replacing the original master cylinder. We disconnected the master cylinder and combination valve to have better access to mount the booster. Plus, the master cylinder needs to be bench bled before installation.

Take the time to bench bleed your master cylinder to remove trapped air bubbles in the internal passages. A syringe can help with the bleeding process when brake fluid is pushed under pressure into the master cylinder's supply passages. The master cylinder is then bolted directly to the brake booster and the brake lines are reattached.

The intake manifold of the small-block had a port for a vacuum source right behind the carburetor mounting flange. Be sure to connect the booster to a manifold vacuum source because most boosters require 18 inches of vacuum as a rule of thumb to function properly.

Banjo Fittings

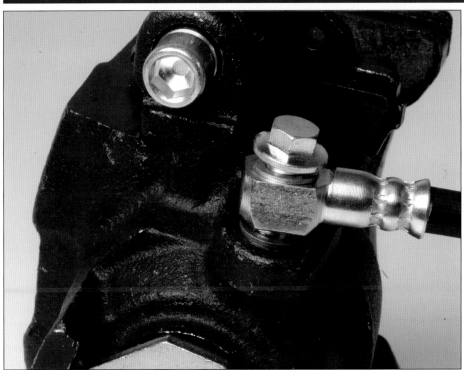

When connecting the rubber hose to the caliper via a banjo fitting, copper compression washers must be used on both sides. Also, note the offset of the fitting. Always ensure that the notched side of the fitting faces outward. Failure to position it correctly could cause a leak.

FORD DISC BRAKE CONVERSION: STREET/STRIP UPGRADE

In the muscle car arms race of the 1960s, Ford had a slow start with heavy and underpowered family street cars. The full-size Ford Galaxie held its own with anything that the other manufacturers put forth. However, midsize Fords struggled to catch up. When they did, it was a fight to claim the title of the baddest and most powerful pavement-tattooing machines on the planet. Braking performance was lagging as the automaker rushed to catch up with its competitors.

These early Ford and Mercury muscle cars were fitted with engines that could achieve 0–60 mph in 6 seconds, but stopping at 60 mph in under 6 seconds with factory brakes was nearly impossible. If you were lucky enough to have the factory disc brake option, braking still suffered if you applied the brakes hard several times in a short period. These would heat up and fade, eventually leaving the driver feeling as if there were no brakes at all.

The Dearborn, Michigan–based company began offering front disc brakes on domestic models as an option in 1965, starting with the Falcon, Thunderbird, Mustang, and Lincoln Continental models. Ford added the front disc brake option on full-size Ford and Mercury models in 1966. This continued with the front disc brake option and rear drums into the 1970s with some midsize models fitted with OEM drums until 1975.

This Ford Falcon Ranchero is representative of the early 1960s Ford economy and intermediate models. These were adequate for the time, but when enthusiasts got their hands on them and injected more power, the stock brakes were simply insufficient and demanded an upgrade.

Even into the late 1970s and early 1980s the stock brakes were only acceptable for moderate street use. Drivers looking for higher performance were forced to seek aftermarket help.

Today, a plethora of disc brake upgrade options are available for classic Ford muscle cars, and they are as varied as the choices of wheels for these iconic machines. The choice of which upgrade to select truly depends on the application and budget.

Options are available from a very basic upgrade that is limited to installing larger brake drums to a simple budget upgrade focused on a front disc brake conversion with OEM-style parts or a high-performance four-wheel, large rotor, six-piston caliper conversion kit and everything in between.

We'll take a look at the original equipment installed at the factory and which part interchanges can be done with these stock-style parts. Then, we'll look at a four-wheel performance disc brake upgrade on a Torino, using a Wilwood disc brake kit.

Vehicle Interchanges/ Crossovers

Ford's "Whiz Kids" developed a financial management control system to help the company control costs, a strategy that contributed to the company's long-running practice of parts standardization. That means suspension and brake parts needed for disc brake conversions, such as spindles and calipers, were standardized to keep costs down. This makes home-built conversions an easier task than some of the other muscle car choices.

The simplest of these OEM junkyard swaps is to use a larger brake drum sourced from station wagons, taxis, police cars, or other high-performance cars. Many of these are equipped with the larger 3-inch-wide front brake drums. These specialty and fleet vehicles have become very popular in recent years, and finding one in a wrecking yard with the parts you want is very unlikely. You can buy stock replacement parts, but it will likely cost you as much as a budget disc brake conversion kit and not perform as well.

Piecing together a front disc brake conversion kit using factory parts from different years and car models can be inexpensive and intensely satisfying, but mixing and matching parts requires careful research and some mechanical experience. When it is done correctly, an OEM-style front disc brake conversion from drum brakes to 11- or 12-inch rotors will dramatically increase performance and likely impress everyone in your car club. After all, anyone can follow instructions in a kit and bolt on matched parts.

One of the most popular OEM front brake conversions for the Ford Mustang is accomplished with parts from the late-1970s Ford Granada. The Granada entered the market as a replacement for the Ford

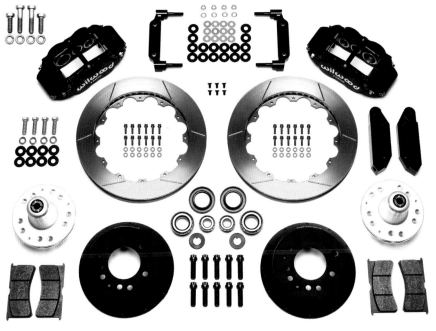

For this full brake system upgrade on a 1968 Ford Torino, the Wilwood Superlite 6 Big Brake Front Brake Kit with 12.88-inch vented rotors (part number 140-10219) was chosen due to the kit's popularity. (Photo Courtesy Wilwood Engineering Inc.)

To match the front braking upgrade, the Wilwood Dynalite Rear Parking Brake Kit with 12.19-inch, 2.5-inch offset vented rotors (part number 140-7140) was chosen to complete the four-wheel brake improvement. (Photo Courtesy Wilwood Engineering Inc.)

Maverick, designed as a step-up vehicle for families that wanted something more than a compact car. This humble urban commuter ended up earning accolades for dependability and was popular enough for the manufacturer to build more than two million for the domestic market in its seven-year production run.

Grenada Front Brake Swap on Mustang

The Grenada front brake swap has been successfully accomplished on Mustangs ranging from 1964 to 1973. Mustang enthusiasts attempting this down-and-dirty swap will need to source a few components from a wrecking yard or retail parts store, including spindles, backing plates, rotors, calipers, mounting hardware, rubber brake lines, a proportioning valve, and steel brake lines.

While the upper and lower ball joints do not need to be swapped as part of the disc brake conversion, it is a good idea to inspect and replace the ball joint if any wear is detected. Replacing the inner and outer bearings is another smart move when replacing the rotor. New brake pads are also a wise investment and the rotors should be resurfaced for optimal performance.

Spindles sourced from 1963–1965 Falcons and 1965–1966 Mustangs work well with Granada calipers and rotors, but they can be difficult to find in salvage yards. The 1966 Falcons, 1967–1973 Mustangs, and 1974–1980 Maverick/Granada/Monarchs support the steering geometry suited for this conversion and are the preferable choice. In addition to proper steering geometry, these spindles have identical ball joints, making the swap easier.

For mounting the calipers in this conversion, a mounting bracket from the same donor car the calipers are taken from will need to be used. Many of these were add-on brackets for optional disc brakes. From 1968 through 1973, the Maverick used a disc brake knuckle engineered specifically for disc brake systems. These are a good choice for the conversion as well.

Rotor selection is important because they will not all fit on Mustangs or other classic midsize Fords. Rotors marked with the "MIN. THICKNESS .810" are the discs used in this swap. Use caution for the rotors that look similar but have thickness of 1 inch or more. These will not work on Mustangs or other midsize Fords. Make sure to have the rotors checked and surfaced before using them.

Many of these rotors were very close to discard specs when they were originally manufactured. Modern replacement discs are available and a great option. Other new parts to consider are brake pads, rebuilt calipers, hoses, wheel bearings, cotter pins, hardware, and tie-rods. Brake fluid, a master cylinder, and new steel brake lines will also be required. The easiest choice for a master cylinder is to use one from the donor car that provided most of the other parts. It is highly recommended that you upgrade your proportioning valve along with this conversion.

Start by removing the drum brakes and spindles along with the brake master cylinder and brake distribution block. If you have to replace the outer tie-rods with a set that matches the replacement spindle, remove the old outer tie-rod ends. Replace those parts with the disc brake parts that you have sourced.

This Ford spindle is typical of the stock 1968–1969 stock Ford disc spindles. The disc spindles are easily identified by the three-bolt back plate mounting bosses. (Photo Courtesy Baer Brakes)

This spindle is typical of the 1970 Ford drum spindles. The back plate is secured with four bolts, which gives this spindle its name: the four-bolt Ford spindle. (Photo Courtesy Baer Brakes)

This mid-1970s Ford Granada rotor and caliper are fitted onto the stock spindle and mounted on a 1965 Ford Mustang. Once considered an inexpensive and easy front disc brake swap, these parts have become increasingly difficult to find in wrecking yards.

Tips on Sourcing Parts from Wrecking Yards

For parts such as calipers and valves, attempt to recover parts that have fluid in the system. This will lessen the chance of buying a component with dried seals that will leak.

When sourcing and removing proportioning valves or other valves, don't risk damaging the valve by attempting to loosen the flare nuts in the donor vehicle. Instead, simply cut the brake lines 1 to 2 inches away from the valve with side cutters. This will make the line removal much easier in your home garage with a vise and proper tools.

Many of the steel brake lines on the front have coiled wire wrapped around them to keep the lines located properly. It is smart to reuse these coiled wires on your new brake lines. To remove and reuse these wire coils, just cut the old brake lines with side cutters and pull the wires off the old brake lines. They can easily be installed on your new brake lines while they are off the vehicle. ■

Ford Disc Brake Spindle Interchange

Part Number	Side	Year and Model
C7SZ 3105-A	R/H	1966–1977 Ford, 1966–1977 Mercury, 1967 Thunderbird
C6AA 3107C	R/H	
C7AA 3107B	R/H	
C7SZ 3106-A	L/H	
C6AA 3108C	L/H	
C7AA 3108B	L/H	
C8SZ 3106-A	R/H	1968 Ford, 1968 Mercury, 1969 Mark III, 1968 Thunderbird
C8SA 3107B	R/H	
C8SZ 3106-A	L/H	
C8SA 3108B	L/H	
D2AZ 3105-B	R/H	1965 Fairlane, 1969–1972 Ford, 1969–1971 Mark III, 1969–1971 Mercury, 1969–1971 Thunderbird
D2AZ 3106-B	L/H	
D0SA 3107A	R/H	
D2AA 3107 BA, BB	R/H	
D0SA 3108A	L/H	
D2AA 3108 BA, BB	L/H	
C90Z 3105C	R/H	1967 Comet/Montego, 1967 Falcon, 1967 Fairlane, 1967 Cougar, 1967 Mustang; 4-bolt spindle
C90Z 3106C	L/H	
C80Z 3105A	R/H	1968–1969 Comet/Montego, 1968–1969 Cougar, 1968–1970 Falcon, 1968–1969 Fairlane, 1968–1970 Mustang
C80Z 3105A	L/H	
D00Z 3105B	R/H	1970 Comet/Montego, 1970 Cougar, 1970 Fairlane, 1971 Montego, 1970 Mustang, 1971 Torino
D0ZA 3107C	R/H	
D00Z 3106B	L/H	
D0ZA 3108C	L/H	
D20Z 3105B	R/H	1972 Fairlane, 1973 Ford, 1973 Mercury, 1972–1973 Montego, 1972–1973 Thunderbird, 1972–1973 Torino; 3-bolt spindle
D20A 3107-AE, BA	R/H	
D20Z 3106B	L/H	
D20A 3108-AE, BA	L/H	
D1ZZ 3105A	R/H	1971–1973 Cougar, 1971–1973 Mustang
D1ZA 3107AA	R/H	
D1ZZ 3106A	L/H	
D1ZA 3108AA	L/H	
C5SZ 3105A	R/H	1965–1966 Thunderbird
C5SZ 3106A	L/H	
D4AZ 3105A	R/H	1974–1976 Cougar, 1974–1978 Ford, 1974–1979 Mark III and IV, 1974–1978 Mercury, 1974–1976 Montego, 1974–1979 Thunderbird, 1974–1976 Torino
D4AZ 3106A	L/H	
D5FZ 3105A	R/H	1974 Bobcat, 1974–1979 Pinto, 1974–1978 Mustang
D5FZ 3106A	L/H	
D4DZ 3105A	R/H	1973–1974 Comet, 1974 Maverick
D4DZ 3106A	L/H	
D4VY 3105A	R/H	1974–1979 Lincoln
D4VY 3105A	L/H	

Ford Disc Brake Calipers

During this period, Ford only manufactured 10 caliper pairs (left and right) for all makes and models of passenger cars. Add that to the four pairs of calipers for pickup trucks under one ton, for a grand total of 14 right-side and 14 left-side calipers.

A brake caliper production change in the 1970s replaced the threaded hose connections with a banjo-style connection that had soft copper washers for a seal. Careful attention to the caliper and hose combination must be used when performing a caliper swap with donor cars from the mid-1970s.

Kelsey-Hayes became a pioneer in disc brake systems early in the 1960s. Its innovations led its systems to become standard equipment on Lincoln Continentals and other Ford models. By the early 1970s, Kelsey-Hayes disc brakes were fitting on 85 percent of US cars. It became the number one brake supplier to Ford, replacing Bendix.

The early model years when disc brakes were optional (1965–1967) have very few interchanges. The Caliper Interchange table outlines the direct caliper interchanges for the nameplates that offered front disc brakes as an option.

As we mentioned previously, the Ford Granada front disc brake swap is one of the most popular OEM-style disc brake conversions for early Ford muscle car enthusiasts. The foundation for a Granada front disc brake swap is the front spindle, which has multiple applications. The single-piston caliper and 11-inch rotor works well for stopping heavier sedans, while still maintain-

Ford Caliper Interchange		
Part Number	**Side**	**Year and Model**
C5SZ 2B120G	R/H	1965–1966 Ford, 1965–1966 Lincoln, 1965–1966 Mercury, 1965–1966 Thunderbird
C5SZ 2B121G	L/H	
C7SZ 2B120A	R/H	1966–1967 Ford, 1967–1969 Lincoln, 1967 Mercury, 1966–1967 Thunderbird
C7SZ 2B121A	L/H	
C5SZ 2B120G	R/H	1965–1966 Ford, 1965–1966 Lincoln, 1965–1966 Mercury, 1965–1966 Thunderbird
C5SZ 2B121G	L/H	
C7SZ 2B120A	R/H	1966–1967 Ford, 1967–1969 Lincoln, 1967 Mercury, 1966–1967 Thunderbird
C7SZ 2B121A	L/H	
C8AZ 2B120A	R/H	1968–1972 Ford, 1970–1972 Lincoln, 1968–1972 Mercury, 1969–1971 Mark III, 1968–1971 Thunderbird
C8AZ 2B121A	L/H	
D20Z 2B120A	R/H	1974–1975 Cougar, 1973–1975 Ford, 1973 Lincoln, 1972–1974 Mark IV, 1973–1974 Mercury, 1972–1976 Montego, 1972–1973 Thunderbird, 1972–1975 Torino
D20Z 2B121A	L/H	
C5ZZ 2B120C	R/H	1965–1966 Mustang
C5ZZ 2B121C	L/H	
C70Z 2B120C	R/H	1967 Comet, 1967 Cougar, 1967 Fairlane, 1967 Falcon, 1967 Mustang
C70Z 2B120C	L/H	
C80Z 2B120A	R/H	1968–1973 Cougar, 1968–1971 Comet/Montego, 1968–1970 Fairlane, 1968–1970 Falcon, 1968–1973 Mustang, 1971 Torino
C80Z 2B120A	L/H	
D1FZ 2B120C	R/H	1971–1973 Pinto
D1FZ 2B121C	L/H	
D4VY 2B120A	R/H	1974–1979 Lincoln, 1974–1979 Mark IV, 1974–1978 Mercury, 1974–1979 Thunderbird
D4VY 2B121A	L/H	
D4FZ 2B120A	R/H	1974 Bobcat, 1974 Comet, 1974 Pinto, 1974–1975 Maverick, 1974–1975 Mustang
D4FZ 2B121A	L/H	

Using sourced components from a donor car allows for the use of factory wheels or aftermarket wheels designed like OEM-style wheels. These wheels fit inside the vehicle's wheel wells without modifications. Larger wheels pose a challenge in keeping the tires tucked within the body.

ing a Ford standard five-bolt wheel lug pattern.

The Granada front disc brake conversion is an easy upgrade swap for the Ford Falcon, Mercury Comet, 1963–1970 Ford Rancheros, most 1964–1973 Mustangs, and 1962–1967 Fairlane models.

If you are working with a 1964–1969 Ford Mustang, Fairlane, or Mercury Comet with five-bolt factory drum brakes, these models have the exact same spindle used in the factory disc brake option. The same spindle was used for both applications in each model year. The factory calipers can be used with factory rotors as an even easier swap.

For 1968 and 1969 Mustangs, Fairlanes, and Comets, the four-piston Kelsey-Hayes caliper with the larger factory 11^{19}/$_{64}$-inch rotors can be used without changing spindles for more stopping power. As an added bonus, this swap can be performed without having to change alignment settings.

The most popular donor cars for the Granada front disc brake swap have been identified as the 1975–1977 Ford Maverick/Mercury Comet and 1975–1980 Ford Granada/Mercury Monarch. Pay attention to the outer tie-rod when performing these swaps. It may be necessary to use the outer tie-rod from the donor car along with the spindle. The inner tie-rod and the tie-rod adjuster sleeve should work with the new outer tie-rod with no issues.

OEM-Style Front Rotors

Typically, Ford intermediates and personal coupes were fitted with rotors that enthusiasts referred to as 10- or 11-inch rotors. Anyone seriously considering stopping power in intermediate-chassis muscle cars will look at the larger rotors. The 10-inch rotors were typically a four-wheel-stud version in a 4.25-inch circular bolt pattern. The 11-inch rotors more commonly found on the Ford intermediate chassis were a five-wheel-stud version on a 4.5-inch circular pattern. These rotors actually measured 11.297 inch in diameter.

These rotors are the same size as the factory Mustang, Fairlane, Montego, Gran Torino, Thunderbird,

Ford Front Rotor Interchange		
Part Number	Year and Model	Details
C5SZ 1102 A	1965–1967 Ford, 1966–1967 Mercury, 1965–1967 Thunderbird	Vented, 5x4.5, 11.720-inch diameter
C8AZ 1102 A	1968 Ford, 1969 Mark III two-piece, 1968 Mercury, 1968 Thunderbird	Vented, 5x4.5, 11.720-inch diameter
C9AZ 1102 A	1969 Mark III one-piece, 1969 Mercury, 1969 Ford, 1969 Thunderbird	Vented, 5x4.5, 11.720-inch diameter
D0AZ 1102 A	1970–1972 Ford, 1970–1972 Lincoln, 1970–1971 Mark III, 1970–1972 Mercury, 1970–1971 Thunderbird	Vented, 5x4.5, 11.720-inch diameter
C5ZZ 1102 B		
C5SZ 1102 B		
C5ZZ 1102 A	1967 Cougar, 1967 Comet, 1967 Fairlane, 1967 Falcon, 1965–1967 Mustang	Vented, 5x4.5, 11.297-inch diameter
C80Z 1120 A	1968–1969 Cougar, 1968–1969 Comet/Montego, 1968–1969 Fairlane, 1968–1970 Falcon, 1968–1969 Mustang	Vented, 5x4.5, 11.297-inch diameter
D00Z 1102 B	1972–1973 Montego with 14-inch wheels, 1972 Torino with 14-inch wheels	Vented, 5x4.5, 11.297-inch diameter
D2SZ 1102 A	1972 Montego with 15-inch wheels, 1972 Mark IV, 1972 Torino with 15-inch wheels, 1972 Thunderbird	Vented, 5x4.5, 11.720-inch diameter
D1FZ 1102 B	1971 and up Mustang with manual transmission	Vented, 4x4.25, 9.30-inch diameter
C5VY 1102 C	1965–1969 Lincoln	
D3AZ 1102 A		
D30Z 1102 A	1973 Ford, 1973, Lincoln, 1973 Mark IV, 1973 Mercury, 1973 Montego with 15-inch wheels, 1973 Torino (11^{13}/$_{16}$ rotor), 1973 Thunderbird	Vented, 5x5, 11.720-inch diameter
D6MY 1102 A	1974–1978 Ford, 1974–1976 Mercury (11^{13}/$_{16}$ rotor), 1974–1976 Montego (11^{13}/$_{16}$ rotor), 1974–1976 Torino (11^{13}/$_{16}$ rotor)	Vented, 5x5, 11.720-inch diameter
D60Z 1102 A	1974–1979 Cougar (10^{3}/$_{4}$ rotor), 1974–1976 Montego (10^{3}/$_{4}$ rotor), 1977–1979 Thunderbird, 1974–1976 Torino (10^{3}/$_{4}$ rotor)	Vented, 5x4.5, 11.720-inch diameter

and some Cougar models offered in the mid-1960s. Many of the Ford models came with 14-inch wheels from the factory. Converting to front disc brakes using the stock-style 11.297-inch disc should yield great results. These rotors should clear those factory-style wheels of the same era. There can be some exceptions, such as using the 11.297-inch rotors with aftermarket forged-aluminum calipers.

It wasn't long before home builders figured out that the 11.720-inch-diameter rotors (often referred to as 12-inch rotors) with calipers and hardware from the full-size Fords would interchange with the 11-inch rotors. Most of these were fitted with 15-inch factory wheels.

You must use the caliper brackets, wheel bearings, and seals for these cars with the larger discs. Because the 12-inch rotors have the 5x5-inch bolt pattern and almost all intermediate chassis cars from this era used a 5x4.5-inch bolt pattern, you must use the 1972 Thunderbird 12-inch rotor with the 5x4.5-inch bolt pattern with the intermediate spindles to maintain the same wheel bolt pattern on the front and rear. Otherwise, be prepared to change the rear axles to make it match. The bearings on the 1972 Thunderbird spindles are the same as the 12-inch rotors.

Ford Factory Wheels		
Size	Bolt Pattern	Year and Model
13x4.00	4x4.50	1974 Bobcat, 1960–1965 Falcon, 1971–1974 Pinto, 1974 Mustang
13x4.50	4x4.50	1960–1963 Comet, 1971 Comet, 1964–1966 Falcon, 1965–1966 Mustang, 1970–1971 Maverick
13x4.50	5x4.50	1963 Comet, 1962–1964 Fairlane, 1960–1964 Falcon
13x5.00	4x4.50	1974–1976 Bobcat, 1974 Mustang, 1971–1974 Pinto
13x5.50	4x4.50	1974–1976 Bobcat, 1974 Pinto, 1974–1975 Mustang
14x4.50	4x4.50	1964–1965 Comet, 1967 Comet, 1964–1967 Falcon, 1970–1972 Maverick, 1965–1967 Mustang
14x4.50	5x4.50	1971–1974 Comet, 1961–1964 Ford, 1966–1967 Fairlane, 1971–1974 Maverick
14x5.00	5x4.50	1963–1972 Comet, 1967–1979 Cougar, 1963–1970 Falcon, 1962–1970 Fairlane, 1973–1974 Montego, 1965–1969 Mustang, 1971–1972 Torino
14x5.50	5x4.50	1966–1970 Comet, 1967–1969 Cougar, 1972–1973 Comet, 1973–1974 Cougar, 1966–1967 Fairlane, 1963–1964 Ford, 1973 Maverick, 1973–1976 Montego, 1961–1964 Mercury, 1967 Mustang, 1973 Mustang, 1962–1964 Thunderbird, 1972–1974 Torino, 1972–1974 Ranchero
14x6.00	4x4.50	1970–1972 Maverick
14x6.00	5x4.50	1968–1969 Comet, 1967–1973 Cougar, 1961–1964 Ford, 1961–1963 Lincoln, 1968–1969 Fairlane, 1961–1964 Mercury, 1972–1976 Montego, 1971–1974 Maverick, 1965–1973 Mustang
14x7.00	5x4.50	1971–1974 Cougar, 1970 Fairlane, 1970–1971 Montego, 1973–1976 Montego, 1970–1972 Mustang, 1971–1974 Torino
15x7.00	5x4.50	1971–1972 Cougar, 1970 Fairlane, 1969–1973 Mustang, 1971 Torino
15x6.00	5x4.50	1965–1972 Ford, 1964–1972 Lincoln, 1969–1972 Mark III, 1965–1971 Mercury, 1972 Montego, 1970–1972 Thunderbird, 1972–1974 Torino
15x5.00	5x4.50	1965–1972 Ford, 1965–1972 Mercury
15x5.50	5x4.50	1961–1972 Ford, 1965–1966 Mustang, 1962–1964 Mercury, 1968–1972 Mercury, 1964–1969 Thunderbird
15x6.50	5x4.50	1969–1972 Ford, 1969–1972 Mercury, 1974 Torino
15x5.00	5x5.00	1973–1974 Ford, 1973–1975 Mercury
15x5.50	5x5.00	1973–1975 Ford
15x6.00	5x5.00	1973–1977 Ford, 1973–1976 Lincoln, 1973–1978 Mark IV-Mark V, 1973–1976 Mercury, 1973 Montego, 1973–1974 Thunderbird, 1973 Torino
15x6.50	5x5.00	1973–1978 Ford, 1973–1976 Mercury, 1973–1976 Montego, 1973–1974 Torino

Ford Master Cylinder Interchange

Part Number	Year and Model	Details
C5AZ 2140A	1964 Comet, 1964 Falcon, 1964–1965 Fairlane, 1964–1965 Ford, 1964–1965 Mercury, 1965 Mustang	1-inch diameter; manual brakes
C7AZ 2140K	1967 Ford, 1967 Mercury	1-inch diameter; power brakes
C7AZ 2140L	1967–1968 Ford, 1967–1968 Mercury	15/16-inch diameter; power brakes
C8AZ 2140B	1968 Ford, 1968 Mercury	1-inch diameter; manual brakes
C7VY 2140A	1968 Ford, 1967–1970 Lincoln, 1968 Mercury	1-inch diameter; power brakes
C9AZ 2140A	1968–1971 Ford, 1969–1971 Mercury	1-inch diameter; power brakes
C9AZ 2140C	1969–1971 Ford	Manual disc brake applications
C9AZ 2140B	1969–1971 Ford, 1970–1971 Mark III, 1969–1971 Mercury, 1970–1971 Thunderbird	1-inch diameter; power brakes
D2AZ 2140A	1972 Ford, 1972 Lincoln, 1972 Mercury	15/16-inch diameter; power brakes
C50Z 2140A	1963–1966 Fairlane	1-inch diameter; power brakes
C60Z 2140B	1966 Comet, 1966 Fairlane, 1966 Falcon	1-inch diameter; power brakes
C60Z 2140D	1966 Comet, 1966 Fairlane, 1966 Falcon	1-inch diameter; power brakes
C80Z 2140A	1967–1970 Comet/Montego, 1967–1970 Fairlane, 1971 Montego, 1971 Torino	15/16-inch diameter; power brakes
C70Z 2140J	1968 Comet/Montego, 1967–1968 Fairlane	1-inch diameter; manual brakes
D20Z 2140A	1972 Montego, 1972–1975 Torino	1-inch diameter; manual brakes
D20Z 2140B	1972 Mark IV, 1972 Montego, 1972 Thunderbird, 1972 Torino	1-inch diameter; power brakes
C1SZ 2140A	1964 Comet, 1964 Falcon, 1964 Ford, 1964 Mercury, 1965 Mustang, 1961–1964 Thunderbird	7/8-inch diameter; power brakes
C5ZZ 2140C	1966 Mustang GT350	15/16-inch diameter; power brakes
C6ZZ 2140C	1966 Mustang (except GT350)	15/16-inch diameter; power brakes
C8ZZ 2140A	1967–1972 Cougar, 1967–1972 Mustang	1-inch diameter; power brakes
C9ZZ 2140B	1969–1970 Mustang	9/16-inch diameter; power brakes
D3ZZ 2140A	1972–1973 Cougar, 1972–1973 Mustang	15/16-inch diameter; power brakes
D1FZ 2140B	1971 Pinto	15/16-inch diameter; manual brakes
D2FZ 2140C	1972 Pinto	15/16-inch diameter
D3FZ 2140A	1972–1973 Pinto	15/16-inch diameter
D2DZ 2140A	1972–1973 Comet, 1972–1973 Maverick	1-inch diameter
D5SZ 2140A	1965–1966 Thunderbird	15/16-inch diameter
C6SZ 2140B	1966 Thunderbird	7/8-inch diameter
C7SZ 2140C	1967 Thunderbird	1-inch diameter
C8SZ 2140A	1969 Mark III, 1968–1969 Thunderbird	1-inch diameter
C5DZ 2140A	1965 Comet, 1965 Falcon	1-inch diameter
C5VY 2140C	1965–1966 Lincoln	1-inch diameter
D1VY 2140B	1971 Lincoln	1-inch diameter
D6AZ 2140A	1974–1979 Cougar, 1973–1975 Ford, 1973–1974 Lincoln, 1973–1974 Mark IV, 1973–1975 Mercury, 1973–1976 Montego, 1973–1974 Thunderbird, 1973–1976 Torino	Power brakes

In many cases, the donor car will have drum brakes on the rear. Pay attention to the bolt pattern and understand the differences in proportioning valves when converting to a disc brake system. Achieving the proper balance in brake effort between the front and rear is critical.

In addition to other major changes in the automotive industry in the mid-1970s, Ford standardized the front wheel bearings (smaller OD inside bearing) on its Ford, Lincoln, and Mercury full- and intermediate-size passenger cars. This makes it easier to use the 12-inch rotor that was more common in the mid-1970s. You will have to source 15-inch wheels with the 5x5 bolt pattern for the conversion to work.

OEM Master Cylinders, Power Units, Proportioning Valves

Like most muscle cars built before regulations that required dual reservoirs were enacted in 1968, vehicles used a single circuit brake system. These were basically a single hydraulic fluid reservoir with a piston. This system would push brake fluid to each wheel when the driver stepped on the brake pedal. Everything worked well until a wheel cylinder or line developed a leak or failed. The entire system was compromised and many times the vehicle was left with no operating brakes after the fluid drained out of the system.

After Department of Transportation regulations required all vehicles to use a dual brake master cylinder, most car companies adopted a master cylinder that was split vertically into two separate chambers, dividing the master cylinder into two circuits: one for the front brakes and one for the rear brake system. If one system were to fail, the other circuit would still operate. This redundant system brought a level of safety to automotive braking that had been sorely lacking. Upgrading the brake system in a muscle car manufactured prior to 1968 would almost certainly benefit from a dual circuit master cylinder.

Aftermarket Conversions

While stock OEM disc brake system upgrades will work very well for the typical daily driver and normal street and highway driving, performance enthusiasts would benefit more from an aftermarket brake manufacturer conversion. Any muscle car owner who competes regularly in racing events or does spirited driving on winding roads tends to push the stock brakes to the limit or beyond their capabilities. Other factors, such as driving styles, performance modifications, and the type of driving can also overcome stock brakes. The question then becomes: What brake system should be used?

Piecing a system together from a wrecking yard can cost you as much as a quality aftermarket upgrade kit, and you don't have to rebuild any components. These aftermarket kits come with specific instructions and are supplied with parts that have been tested for compatibility and performance. With most front brake conversions starting around $500, it makes little sense to spend your time digging through junkyards for parts.

High-Performance 1968 Ford Torino Big Brake Upgrade

Torino had a successful 1968 with 172,083 units produced. Including Fairlane production, 371,787 total cars were produced. The Torino was well received by the press and a 1968 Torino GT convertible was selected as the 1968 Indianapolis 500 pace car due to its styling and power. The stock brakes were barely sufficient at stock engine power, and the braking was horribly inadequate when a highly modified engine was added. In these cases, a brake upgrade is almost always needed not only for performance but also for safety.

Like many Ford muscle cars in the 1960s, these have become project cars for serious gearheads. Often infused with big-cubic-inch engines

with lopey cams, these machines are great candidates for improved braking. The nasty camshafts almost always guarantee low vacuum, which means considerations for power assist are limited. Planning a high-performance brake system for a car like this requires planning and thought. A brake booster will not increase stopping power. It does reduce the pedal effort and is recommended for most midsize and full-size cars when vacuum can be generated for actuation.

Many aftermarket manufacturers offer "big brake kits." It is not uncommon for consumers to ask: What makes a brake kit *big*? We don't mean to oversimplify the math

behind the braking process, but the basic elements are the diameter of the rotor, the size of the caliper, and the coefficient of friction of the brake pads. Of course, there are other components in the systems that can play a role in stopping power. Master cylinder bore size and pedal ratio are two of the most prominent factors. Generally, manufacturers offer larger disks and larger calipers in their big brake kits.

Choosing a Wilwood big brake kit offers a number of benefits for heavier Detroit iron. Bigger brakes and rotors mean increased heat capacity, which is a hedge against brake fade and caliper distortion, especially with multiple stops at higher speed.

Our Wilwood Brake Kit

Selected Components

- Wilwood Superlite 6 Front Brake Kit with 12.88-inch Vented Rotors (part number 140-10219)
- Wilwood Dynalite Rear Parking Brake Kit with 12.19-inch 2.50-inch offset Vented Rotors (part number 140-7140)
- Wilwood Aluminum Tandem Master Cylinder (part number 260-12900 or 260-14157)
- Wilwood Internal Parking Brake Cable Kit (part number 330-9371)

We selected the Wilwood Superlite 6 Front Brake Kit to demonstrate a typical Ford muscle car brake upgrade for higher-performance cars destined for street and strip duty. This Wilwood kit is designed to use factory OEM disc brake spindles, which simplifies the installation and helps keep the cost lower.

The kit also fits a wide range of late 1960s Ford vehicles. These include the 1968–1969 Fairlane, Falcon, Mustang, Ranchero, Torino, Mercury Comet, Mercury Cougar, Mercury Cyclone, and Mercury Montego. The 1970 Ford Mustang GT350 and GT500 are also covered with this kit. There may be other models that will accept this kit as well.

Wilwood's Hamrick advises to call its tech support at 805-388-1188 with any questions. If a factory OEM spindle will not be used, a call to the tech support line may help identify any problems that might be encountered with other aftermarket spindles.

The 6R billet forged six-piston calipers combine with 13-inch slotted rotors for a tandem that supplies more-than-enough braking power for traditional (non-ABS) spindles on Detroit muscle cars. These kits are designed for larger wheels (17-inch and larger) and accommodate performance suspension upgrades typical in these models. Wilwood offers these in a range of options for the enthusiast who wants to individualize his or her project with caliper finishes and rotor designs.

Our demonstration model was outfitted with the base kit with black powder coated calipers and slotted rotors. The calipers (left: part number 120-11781-BK, right: part number 120-11780-BK) are equipped with six stainless steel pistons (one 1.62-inch bore and two 1.12-inch bore) for a total of 4.04 square inches of piston area, and they are coupled with brake pads that have 8.2 square inches of Wilwood's BP-10 pad. ∎

"Stronger and stiffer components offer a firmer pedal with the ability to better modulate the brakes consistently," Wilwood's events and promotions manager, Michael Hamrick, said. "Substantial weight savings in unsprung weight greatly improve driving characteristics by enabling the suspension components to react quicker," he added.

It's well understood that under hard deceleration, a vehicle's weight is transferred to the front, requiring the front brakes to do most of the braking to stop the vehicle. Despite this, adding disc brakes to the rear wheels will improve overall braking performance. Four-wheel disc brakes give the driver the ability to modulate the brakes, increasing braking performance.

To demonstrate how to achieve improved braking performance in vintage muscle cars destined for road racing, autocrossing, or street/strip use, we selected front and rear brake kits from Wilwood. We added a Wilwood master cylinder and parking brake kit to complete the package.

Brake Pad Compound

Brake pads and their material compound are greatly misunderstood by many enthusiasts. Most have the "bigger is better" mentality and think larger pads stop better. The reality is that larger brake pads don't offer more stopping power unless there is more clamping force in the calipers. Larger pads do offer fade resistance because of their size and ability to absorb heat.

Brake pad materials are designed by the manufacturers to work in a certain temperature range. Brake pads designed for everyday street vehicles work well from ambient temperature to around 300°F, while many brake pads designed for heavy-duty racing hardly provide braking at all until they hit 500°F or higher.

Our kit includes calipers loaded with brake pads bearing Wilwood's BP-10 compound. The BP-10 pad compound was developed for high-performance street and strip, drag race, road racing, and oval track usage with vented iron rotors. While compatible with steel or iron rotors, these pads experience low abrasion on iron rotors with medium friction characteristics. That means the BP-10 compound has a low-to-medium wear rate, but like most street pads, wear will increase as temperature increases.

According to Hamrick, choosing a brake pad compound is not as difficult as it may seem. "Temperature range and friction are the top considerations for pad selection," he said. The goal is to select a pad that is able to maintain friction (stopping power) at the temperatures the brakes will operate within. Wear rate should be considered after friction value and temperature range is identified. Wilwood's technical support data provides guidance for wear and heat range in different applications:

- For most asphalt and road race applications, compounds in the high temperature ranges over 1,000°F range are usually necessary.
- Dirt track, drag race, and street performance applications usually operate at temperatures between 500 and 1,000°F.
- Keep in mind that these are general ranges and not absolute values. Many factors and unforeseen influences can affect brake temperatures.

"The best indicator for pad selection will always be on-track performance. If pad fade due to overheating occurs, then improved cooling, a heavier rotor, or a higher-temperature-range pad may all become necessary," advised Hamrick.

Rotors

The rotors in our kit are identified as GT48 curved vane rotors finished in GT slotted style grooves with a plain surface. The "48" in GT48 refers to the number of curved vanes in the rotor. Manufactured out of Wilwood's Spec-37 iron, they measure 12.88 inches in diameter and are referred to as 13-inch rotors. Their measured width is 1.1 inches and the rotors are dynamically balanced for a smooth ride.

There is little doubt that modern disc brakes and rotors are a great improvement over drum brakes. Similar-size drum and disc brakes may stop equally as well, but drum brakes fade quicker. Size means a lot when it comes to deciding which disc kit to use. For example, removing 12-inch drum brakes from a post-war Ford sedan and replacing them with a set of 9-inch Ford pony car rotors may not provide any improvement at all.

In this case, our project car was improved from the factory with 11.25-inch rotors over the standard 10-inch drum brakes. We are replacing the 11.25-inch discs with Wilwood's 13-inch vented iron rotors. There is no doubt that we are making a major performance upgrade. Wilwood specifies a minimum wheel size of 17 inches for these rotors. If there is any lingering doubt, a wheel clearance diagram can be downloaded from the company's webpage. This diagram can be printed and used as a template to check wheel clearance.

Installation

Wheel Clearance Diagram
Kit P/N 140-10219

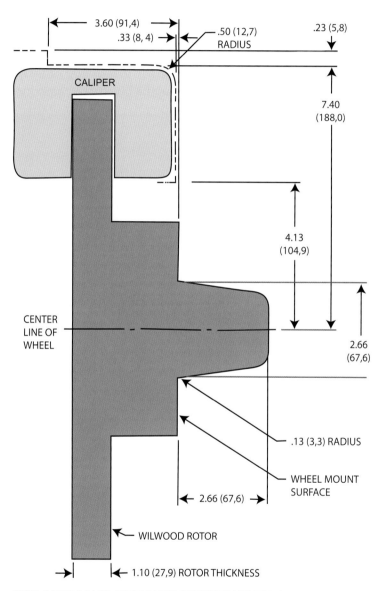

3.60 (91,4)
.33 (8, 4)
.50 (12,7) RADIUS
.23 (5,8)
CALIPER
7.40 (188,0)
4.13 (104,9)
CENTER LINE OF WHEEL
2.66 (67,6)
.13 (3,3) RADIUS
WHEEL MOUNT SURFACE
2.66 (67,6)
WILWOOD ROTOR
1.10 (27,9) ROTOR THICKNESS

NOTE: A MINIMUM OF .080" CLEARANCE MUST BE MAINTAINED
BETWEEN THE WHEEL AND CALIPER IN ALL AREAS

be performed with ease. Outside of a floor jack, jack stands, and a torque wrench, only common hand tools are required.

As with any modifications, there is a chance that the new parts won't fit in the available space. Clearance between the brake caliper and inside of the wheel can be an issue, especially with high-performance braking systems. Reviewing the wheel clearance diagrams before any maintenance is starting will help identify any clearance issues before the vehicle is disassembled. Nothing is more frustrating than a project that is stalled waiting for the correct-size parts.

Stock wheels will not work with this kit, so aftermarket wheels and tires will need to be ordered beforehand. Using the wheel clearance diagram will assist in selecting a set of wheels that will provide sufficient clearance for Wilwood's billet forged Superlite 6 calipers. Additionally, Wilwood's front brake kits generally do not include flex lines. Many of the aftermarket brake kit manufacturers also require the consumer to source flex lines as well.

Due to the age of classic American muscle cars, there is a high possibility that many of the components have been replaced in the decades since the car was new. The differences between like-model vehicles can be huge because of the many variables that exist. It is wise to take a good look at the entire system before any work begins and procure any parts needed to complete the project. This will ensure that the work can be done in one session. Any delays or periods of inactivity can lead to lost parts.

As with most aftermarket brake manufacturers, Wilwood Engineering recommends this installation and any brake maintenance be undertaken by someone experienced with brake systems. If the installer is experienced and possesses decent mechanical skills, installation can

Disassembly

The Wilwood kit uses the stock OEM spindle, and this project vehicle came stock with the front disc brake option, so disassembly was not too difficult. With the front wheels off the ground and the vehicle supported on jack stands, disconnect the brake lines where the flex line ends. To prevent leaking brake fluid from getting on parts or body panels, insert a line plug or fitting into the line coming from the master cylinder reservoir. Remove the stock caliper bracket and OEM caliper assembly.

Removing the stock discs and drums is fairly routine. Remove the center cap, cotter pin, spindle nut, wheel bearing, and washer. The brake rotor and hub assembly should pull off the spindle easily. The OEM spindle on this vehicle is a three-bolt spindle because it is a stock disc brake setup. The three bolts holding the backing (dust) plate need to be removed because the Wilwood kit does not require a dust plate and it will not be reused.

Finally, the caliper bracket can be removed by removing the top and bottom bolts. If any painting or prep work is to be done, now is the best time to clean, prep, and paint the spindles or suspension components. Check the ball joints for wear and ensure that everything is in working order before installing the disc brake components.

The front kit consists of serious 13-inch-diameter, two-piece rotors, new hub assemblies, six-piston calipers, braided brake hoses, bearings, seals, and related hardware for assembly. The Wilwood Superlite 6 Front Brake Kit is suited for a high-performance street car that is capable of daily driving, some spirited street racing, and even some track day driving. While it is a very hardy upgrade, it is not a full-race setup and should not be used as a race-only system. However, it will provide more than adequate service for a weekend warrior. The first step in any installation is to remove all components and lay them out to verify that all parts identified in the instructions are present.

The 1968 Ford Torino was equipped with factory four-wheel, 10-inch drum brakes as the standard, but 11.25-inch front discs were an option along with the power assist. This was also true with the Fairlane, Fairlane 500, and Torino GT.

The brake system needs to match the performance of the car. The stock solid disc and single-piston caliper were adequate for a stock or mildly modified car. However, when in excess of 500 hp, the stock system is underpowered, and this particular Torino exceeds 700 hp. The performance camshaft swap produced low vacuum and was unsuitable for vacuum power-assist braking. Left with few options, it was decided that a manual braking system would provide the best stopping power for this project.

The upgrade began by removing the factory caliper, then the rotor assembly by pulling off the spindle nut cap, cotter pin, and castle nut. It is important to note that, for this installation, the OEM spindle nut will be used with the new rotors.

With the spindle nut and washer removed, the outer wheel bearing can be taken out of the hub. Simply grasp the rotor with both hands and slightly pull the hub outward. The bearing will hang on the end of the spindle, allowing you to remove it with one of your hands. When the bearing is removed, remove the hub and rotor using both hands. It is wise to store these removed components in their own little area off to the side. Decide later if you want to hang on to the original parts, sell them as stock OEM parts, or just scrap them.

Installation of the Wilwood Front Disc Brake Kit

After making sure that all parts are accounted for, the first thing Wilwood recommends in the installation is to check the fitment of the rotor and caliper to the wheels. Even after checking the wheel clearance diagram, check the physical clearance prior to mounting anything to your vehicle. This is the only way to make sure that it will fit properly. If the rotor and caliper don't fit within the wheel with a little bit of clearance, return them since you haven't installed the parts on the car. If the clearance is not acceptable, the rotor and caliper kit or wheel must be changed before the installation can be completed.

The caliper mounting bracket should be assembled and fitment should be checked to make sure it mounts securely against the spindle body. Wilwood recommends doing this with dry threads. Later, the bolts will be removed and coated with red thread locker and torqued to 65 ft-lbs. Using the same three-pass procedure to ensure proper clamping, the first pass should be torqued to 20 ft-lbs. The second pass at 39 ft-lbs, and then the final torque at 65 ft-lbs. This will be done after the caliper has been checked and shimmed for proper alignment to the rotor.

Install the wheel studs into the hub and torque them as directed in the instruction manual. Pack the inner and outer wheel bearings with grease. Then, insert the inner bearing in the hub and install the bearing grease seal in the back of the hub. Insert the outer bearing in the front side of the hub and place the entire hub assembly on the greased spindle snout.

Secure the hub on the spindle with the large washer and spindle nut, then screw on the dust cap. The rotor hat and rotor slide into place over the wheel studs and are secured with three flat-head screws. Finally, the caliper mounting bracket and calipers can be shimmed and torqued to complete the assembly. The brake pads can be inserted into the calipers, and make a quick check to ensure the pads are located correctly on the rotors before moving to the rear disc installation.

Wilwood supplies braided brake hose designed to connect to the factory hard line on the chassis. If your lines are in good shape, the hose can be routed from the caliper to the factory mounting bracket. The factory routing pattern worked for us on the Torino. Make sure that the Wilwood stainless steel lines are long enough for the full suspension travel and route them away from the shocks, sway bar, and suspension components that could interfere with the brake lines. An OEM-style retaining clip secures the line.

1 *Wilwood recommends doing a physical check of the rotor and caliper to ensure a proper fit prior to installing any component. This way the kit can be returned if there is not sufficient clearance. Technically, the brake components have not been installed on the car, but care should be taken to preserve the cosmetic appearance. Install the rotor hat onto the rotor and the hub, then gently place the unit into the wheel shell to check the initial fit. If you are satisfied with the initial check, slide the caliper with brake pads onto the rotor and check the fit again. Wilwood recommends a minimum of 0.080-inch clearance between the wheel and caliper.*

2 *Carefully bolt the rotor hat to the rotor. Not every bolt needs to be installed at this time, just use enough to keep the assembly together and the mating surfaces flush. It is important to use the wheel studs as alignment pins when checking the clearance. Simply place the rotor and rotor hat assembly into the wheel shell and slide the wheel studs through the rotor hat and wheel to align the assembly. Check for any interference.*

3 Take the entire assembly out of the wheel shell and carefully place the Superlite 6 caliper with brake pads onto the rotor. Estimate where the caliper mount will hold the caliper assembly onto the rotor. The caliper pressed onto the rotor should look something like the photo. The entire unit can be reinserted into the wheel shell and once again checked for clearance. If there is a least a minimum of 0.080-inch clearance between the caliper and wheel, the assembly can continue. If not, either the kit or the wheel will need to be changed.

4 After the clearance has been checked and rechecked, the rotor hat can be fully assembled to the rotor. Install all 12 of the 1/4-inch bolts with supplied washers in an alternating sequence, using red thread locker on the bolt's threads. Torque the bolts using a cross-torque method. The final torque value is 155 in-lbs on each bolt. Many professional mechanics start at a lower torque and raise the torque value up to the final torque in a series of torquing passes. The first pass is usually 30 percent of the final torque value. The second pass is 60 percent of the final torque value. The third and final pass is the full torque value. In this case the first pass would be 47 in-lbs, second pass at 93 in-lbs, and the final pass at 155 in-lbs. For an added measure of security, the bolts may be safety wired using standard 0.032-inch-diameter stainless steel safety wire.

5 A bolt-tightening sequence and bolt-torquing sequence is a procedure to ensure proper clamp load of the bolts. The torque values are dependent on the friction between the threads of bolt and nut. This friction can be affected by the application of a lubricant, which in this case is the thread locker. The sequence of tightening is critical to preloading the flanges to be joined. For a 12-bolt flange, the sequence displayed in this diagram is a proven method of torquing and aligning a flange. Care should be used to ensure the flange surfaces are free of dirt, scratches, and tooling marks that would prevent a smooth and flat connection.

6 The torquing process may seem tedious but the extra level of care is required in a system that demands safety to be roadworthy. Using a three-pass sequence of torquing, the clamp load of the bolts is even around the radius of the joint.

Installation of the Wilwood Front Disc Brake Kit *Continued*

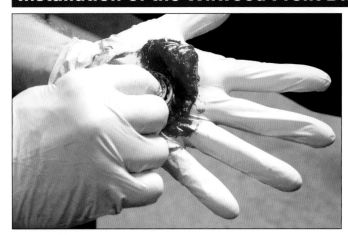

7 The new bearing will not come filled with grease, so pack the bearings yourself. Wilwood recommends a high-temperature disc brake bearing grease when packing the wheel bearings and coating the spindle surfaces. A bearing packing tool is helpful, but if one is not available, the tried-and-true manual method works just as well. High-temperature wheel bearing grease is available at any parts store with some quality products from Lucas Oil, Valvoline, and Sta-Lube on the shelf.

8 Because this kit uses the stock OEM spindles, it is necessary to clean and inspect the spindle looking for any evidence of overheating, damage, or wear. If everything looks good, when you are done packing the inner and outer wheel bearings on the right and left front hubs, liberally coat the machined surfaces of the spindle snout for protection and cooling.

9 Generously apply a layer of the high-temperature disc brake grease inside the hub, don't fill it up, just use a nice layer of grease around the inside of the hub where the spindle goes. Place the inner wheel bearing in the bearing race that is pressed into the hub. Once the hub is installed on the spindle, any excess grease will be pushed out.

10 The grease seal can be placed in the hub housing, but it will need to be pressed into the hub until the outside lip of the seal sits flush with the hub's housing. Most home garage mechanics use a mallet or hammer to tap the grease seal in place. Experienced and well-equipped shops use a floor press to install the seal. A block of wood is preferred over the seal when using a hammer or mallet to seat the seal. The wood block helps to spread the load over the entire seal and prevents the seal from being damaged.

11 Up to this point, we've only had one of the 3/8-16 Torx button head retainers holding the rotor hat to the hub. Now is the time to secure the hub to the rotor assembly by using the other two beefier retainers. Use a dab of red thread locker and torque the bolts to 45 ft-lbs.

12 Slide the hub and rotor assembly onto the spindle and secure it in place with the spindle washer and spindle nut. Finding the correct preload for the bearing by using the spindle nut is an art based on feel. Slowly tighten the spindle nut while turning the rotor. When the rotor starts to bind slightly, the bearing is seated properly. Turn the spindle nut in a loosening direction 1/6 to 1/4 of a turn.

13 Ensure there is no binding after backing off the spindle nut. If the adjusting nut is not backed off there is a possibility of the bearing overheating due to friction. If the bearing fails, the rotor, hub, and wheel could fail to operate properly and become uncontrollable. At this point, the spindle nut can be secured with a cotter pin.

14 Now it's time to add the calipers. This kit uses distinct right-hand and left-hand calipers that must be mounted in specific locations. Start by installing the radial caliper mount bracket to the caliper mount bracket with two 0.030-inch-thick shims between the two mounting surfaces and tighten the bolts temporarily. Mount the assembly to the spindle. The studs on the radial caliper mount bracket will be pointing up if assembled correctly.

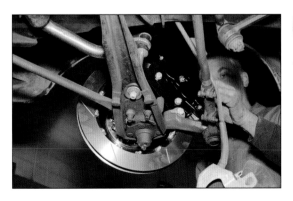

15 The two caliper mounting studs should be lubricated with oil; then, place one 0.035-inch shim on each stud. The caliper is then placed on the mounting studs and secured with a washer and lock nuts. Check to make sure the caliper has the largest pistons at the back (in relationship to the direction of rotation). Look through the top opening of the caliper at the rotor to verify that the rotor is centered inside the caliper. If the rotor is not centered, add or remove shims between the radial caliper mount and flat bracket mount on the spindle as necessary to center the rotor. Wilwood advises to always use the same amount of shims on each of the two mounting bolts.

Installation of the Wilwood Front Disc Brake Kit *Continued*

16 Once the rotor-to-caliper alignment is centered correctly, remove the bolts one at a time, apply red thread locker to the bolt threads, and torque the bolts to 42 ft-lbs.

17 Adding the brake pads and checking the radial alignment of the brake pads on the rotor is the final step to set up this front disc brake conversion. With the caliper aligned and torqued in place, the brake pads drop in from the top. The pads should install easily without interference, so push them into position on both sides of the disc. They are secured in place with the long Allen-head bolt and tube assembly. Add or subtract shims between the caliper and the radial mount bracket to achieve proper alignment. Reinstall the caliper and torque it to 30 ft-lbs.

18 Reinstall the center bridge pad retainer tube, bolt, and locknut. The locknut should be snug without play in the bolt or tube. Do not overtighten it.

Wilwood supplies braided brake hose that is designed to connect to the factory hard line on the chassis. If the lines are in good shape, the hose can be routed from the caliper to the factory mounting bracket. The factory routing pattern worked for us on the Torino. Make sure that the Wilwood stainless steel lines are long enough for the full suspension travel and route them away from the shocks, sway bar, and any suspension components that could interfere with the brake lines. An OEM-style retaining clip secures the line.

Rear Axle Brake Kit

Wilwood's Dynalite New Style Big Bearing Rear Brake Kit with parking brake (part number 140-7140) was perfect for our demonstration vehicle. Originally, the 1968 Ford Torino GT models came with either an 8- or 9-inch rear end housing. Telling the two apart is fairly simple. Looking at the rear end from the back of the vehicle, an 8-inch Ford rear end has a smooth housing, while a 9-inch has a hump.

Our project car was retrofitted with one of the most popular Ford 9-inch rear ends, often referred to by enthusiasts as "new style big Ford" or the "Torino axle" version. Later versions were equipped from the factory with disc brakes. Ours came with the 10-inch drums. The nice thing about the Wilwood rear brake kit design is that most of the original rear end components are retained, only the brakes and backing plates are changed. This means the axles, bearings, flanges, and the housing all remain untouched.

Many enthusiasts ignore parking brake setups in the misbelief that they are not worth the effort. The Wilwood rear brake kit not only makes it easy to install a parking brake setup, they are not very expensive either. Consider it cheap insurance when parking on inclines.

Installation

Once again, it pays to check over the kit, lay out all the parts, and verify them against the packing list in the instructions. Wilwood also recommends measuring the bearing outside diameter and axle housing flange to make sure everything will fit together perfectly. Follow the instructions in the kit to measure the flange dimensions properly.

Installation is as simple as removing the original brake components by raising the car off of the ground and supporting it with jack stands or a lift. Strip the brake drum assembly down to the bare axle. The stock bearing retainers need to be removed, requiring the axle to be slightly pulled out of the housing. This is a great opportunity to inspect the axle flange for any burrs or nicks that could cause a sealing problem.

The mounting bracket, which also contains the parking brake's shoes and hardware, is orientated with the caliper mount facing the rear. Slide the mounting bracket onto the axle, then insert the axle and bracket into the rear end housing. Make sure that the bracket assembly backing plate fits flush against the housing flange.

Install the new bearing retainer with the opening pointing up and the lip facing inward. Use the stock bolts and nuts with red thread locker to secure the retainer to the axle housing flange. Using the rotor register adapter, align the rotor hat with the stud pattern on the axle flange. Install three lug nuts to hold the assembly in place. Then mount caliper into place on the mounting bracket with an initial shim stack-up of two 0.035-inch shims on each bolt between the caliper and the bracket.

As with the front caliper centering, tighten the rear caliper mounting bolts and check the rotor through the top of the caliper. Add or remove shims to center the caliper on the rotor. Make sure to use the same amount of shims on both of the mounting bolts.

Remove the bolts one at a time, apply red thread locker, and torque them to 40 ft-lbs. Load the disc brake pads in the caliper and secure them with the pad clip retainer. Remove the rubber grommet in the back of the bracket assembly and adjust the parking brake shoes while spinning the rotor until a slight drag is felt against the drum portion of the rotor hat. Replace the grommet and install the wheel and lug nuts, making sure the wheel spins freely before moving to the parking brake cable installation.

Rear Brake Installation

1 The rear brake kit consists of 12-inch rotors, inner-drum parking brake assemblies, four-piston calipers, braided brake hoses, and parking brake cables. In most applications, a master cylinder upgrade will be required, complemented by a pre-plumbed combination/proportioning valve assembly. This is the Wilwood Dynalite Rear Parking Brake Kit (part number 140-7140) with 12.19-inch-diameter vented rotors (2.50 offset). The Wilwood Internal Parking Brake Cable Kit (part number 330-9371) was selected for the parking brake cable installation. For the master cylinder upgrade, the Wilwood Aluminum Tandem Master Cylinder (part number 260-12900) was used.

2 Moving to the rear suspension and brakes, the first order of business is to remove the antiquated stock drum brakes. On a Ford 9-inch rear end, the axles are retained by four bolts and a retaining plate behind the mounting flange. As you can see in this application, the retaining plate bolts are behind the axle shaft hub, so the only tool that will fit behind it is a combination wrench. Some Ford axles have a hole in the axle flange so that you can use a conventional ratchet, extension, and socket to remove the retaining plate bolts.

3 Remove the axle shaft at this stage. With the four bolts and retainer plate removed, attach the end plate to the axle shaft hub using the three lug nuts. A slide hammer is used to disengage the axle from the rear end assembly. In most cases with a little quibbling, the axle will slide right out. After removing the axle, remove the backing plate and the remaining brake hardware.

4 After cleaning the axle flange, the Wilwood parking brake assembly and caliper bracket was installed directly to the axle tube. There is no need for a gasket at this flange and none is included in the kit. Note the location of the caliper mount. This positions the rear caliper at the rear of the rotor. The retainer/mount bolts are holding the parking brake assembly and mount in place for this photo. These will be removed when the axle is slid into the axle tube and the bearing retainer is installed.

5 With the caliper bracket assembly and emergency brake installed, carefully support the axles and slide them back into the housing. Use care when sliding the axle splines past the seal and down the axle tube. The seal can be torn or ripped if caution is not used.

6 The retaining bracket slides behind the hub and in front of the axle bearing. It is easiest to insert the retainer bracket with the opening facing down. Then, reorient the bracket so the opening faces up and the lip faces toward the bearing. Torque down the four retaining bolts to secure the axle shaft in place.

7 The factory hard brake line has been retained and will be reused once the new caliper is mounted. It is wise to keep the end of the brake line covered to prevent any debris from getting into the open line.

Rear Brake Installation *Continued*

8 The rear rotors are drilled for multiple bolt patterns. Identify the wheel stud pattern and mark it for ease of installation. Note that these hub assemblies have three bolt patterns. The 5x4.5 is primarily for Ford cars and 5x4.75 is primarily for GM cars. For the Torino and most Ford muscle cars, the 5x4.5 is the correct choice. The 5x5.0 pattern is a performance bolt pattern used in track cars.

9 The Wilwood kit is supplied with a 3.06-inch center ID register (and a 2.80-inch register). This ensures the rotor is centered on the axle flange. If you happen to have axles with different dimensions, Wilwood offers a number of precision machined rings available separately. Install the adapter with the smaller outside diameter facing the rotor.

10 Position the caliper over the rotor and line up the mounting holes. Use two 0.035-inch shims between the caliper and the bracket and tighten the mounting fasteners. Check the position of the rotor in the caliper as you checked on the front. If it's not centered, add or remove shims until the rotor is centered.

11 Once everything is in position, use a touch of red thread locker and torque the bolts to 40 ft-lbs. The brake pads easily slide into place and are secured with the pad clip retainer.

Parking Brake Cable Installation

Install the brake lines provided by Wilwood with the kit, and if the master cylinder is not being changed or other components such as line lock or proportioning valves are not being added, carefully bleed the brakes. Next, ensure that the brake hoses are routed to prevent contact with moving suspension, brake, or wheel components. Finally, perform a safety inspection for function and leaks. Check chapter 7 for inspection pro tips and tricks. In this case, we are adding a master cylinder and proportioning valve. We will be bleeding the brakes as the last step of the entire installation.

Wilwood engineers are quick to point out that maximum performance from your parking brake system is achieved when the cables are routed as straight as possible. Bends in the cable can significantly reduce efficiency and thus reduce pull force at the brake. As with any cable, tight bends must be avoided, and Wilwood's instructions recommend a minimum bend radius of 6 to 8 inches. This is best accomplished by uncoiling the parking brake cable and laying it out flat. Then, remove the parking brake cable from the cable cover and pull the cable completely out.

Locate the parking brake lever clevis, insert the non-ball end of the cable through the center hole of the

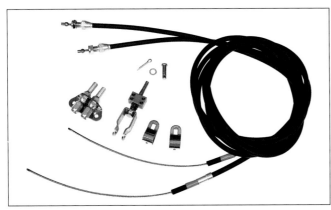

1 Wilwood's Internal Parking Brake Cable Kit (part number 330-9371) is designed for use with Wilwood's forged Dynalite and billet Superlite 4 internal parking brake kits. The kit is fairly straightforward and easy to install. This kit is like the OEM parking brake cable system, but it is built a little more stout and is adjustable. (Photo Courtesy Wilwood Engineering Inc.)

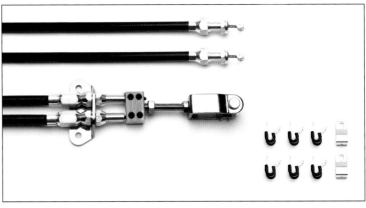

2 The Wilwood parking brake cable has an inner brake cable end with a ball swaged onto the end that seats into the clevis that attaches to the parking brake lever. This inner cable must be pulled out of the outer housing to route the cable through the clevis and reinserted back into the cable housing. The other end of the cable is inserted into the junction block that attaches to the parking brake actuator. (Photo Courtesy Wilwood Engineering Inc.)

3 The cables are made longer than needed to fit multiple applications and need to be custom fit for each individual application. We measured the cable for fit and cut the cables with a rotary tool for a clean, easy to work with, cut cable end. These ends slipped into the junction housing easily.

Parking Brake Cable Installation *Continued*

clevis, and pull the cable until the ball is secure against the inside face of the clevis. Reinsert the cable into the cable cover and feed it all the way back through.

Slide the slot in the clevis over the parking brake lever, slide the cable end fitting into the slot on the cable stop bracket, and snug down the supplied 7/16-inch lock nut. Another important Wilwood recommendation is to use anti-seize lubricant on aluminum nuts like this lock nut.

Route the cables forward, tracing the OEM stock cable route exactly. This ensures the cable will operate correctly without any obstructions, bends, kinks, or other issues. Use care to route lines to prevent contact with the exhaust, moving suspension, and brake and wheel components. Repeat these steps for the other rear tire parking brake assembly.

After the cables have been attached at both rear parking brake levers, route both cables forward and slide the housing end adjuster over the two inner cables until it bottoms out against the cable covers. Slide the ferrules into the housing end adjuster with a drop of red thread locker to hold it in position.

Slide the cables into the cable block assembly and attach the cable block clevis to the parking brake. Follow the instructions provided with the cable kit for adjusting the cable tension and parking brake final adjustments.

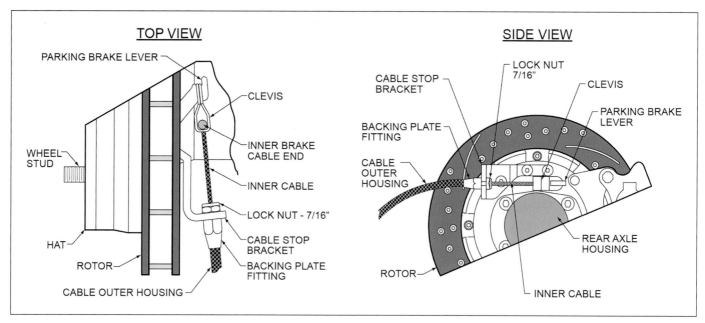

4 The image above shows how the cable fits into the parking brake lever and the cable end fitting slides into the slot on the cable stop bracket to be secured by a 7/16-inch lock nut. (Illustration Courtesy Wilwood Engineering Inc.)

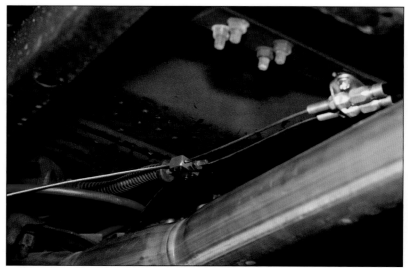

5 The junction block is shown after the cables from each wheel have been routed to the parking brake actuator. The final adjustment will be performed when the car is down on the ground with the suspension at ride height.

Master Cylinder Installation

The master cylinder is mounted to the existing holes in the firewall where the original master cylinder was located. The master cylinder kit includes one 9/16-inch, one 1/2-inch, and two 3/8-inch inverted-flare threaded line adapters for connections to the brake lines. These adapters are not installed in the master cylinder at the factory but as added convenience for installers who may need to adapt the master cylinder to older brake line hoses. Two hex head plugs are also supplied by Wilwood to block the unused outlet ports.

Pressure readings or pressure switches can be taken from either side of the master cylinder. After selecting the size and location of the outlet ports to be used, lubricate adapter fitting threads lightly with silicone or lithium-based grease, then install the fittings and plugs, using the aluminum crush washers, and torque each to 20-25 ft-lbs.

Attach the brake pedal's pushrod to the pedal assembly and ensure the brake pedal moves all the way to the stop. The Wilwood tandem master cylinder has a built-in safety feature with the ability to build pressure in one circuit if the other one fails. If a circuit failure occurs, the pedal (pushrod) may travel 50 to 80 percent of the full stroke before starting to build up pressure in the other circuit for emergency stopping.

To make sure this safety feature works properly, ensure the pushrod will bottom out in the bore before installation. Prior to adding brake fluid, test the pushrod for full stroke before the pedal stops against the floorboard. If the pushrod doesn't travel the full 1.10-inch stroke, adjustments need to be made to the

1 *Our project car was originally fitted with a power-assisted brake unit, but the engine had been modified for power with a huge cam that would not produce the vacuum needed to allow the power assist to work properly. We upgraded the system with a Wilwood tandem chamber master cylinder without a power booster unit. (Photo Courtesy Wilwood Engineering Inc.)*

2 *With the new calipers and rotors installed, it is time to move under the hood for the master cylinder update. Remove the brake lines carefully to not drip or splash any fluid on painted components.*

3 *Remove the factory master cylinder along with the original combination valve. Also, remove the four nuts from under the dash to pull the factory booster. While under the dash, disconnect the pushrod and remove the entire unit from the firewall.*

pushrod, pedal, and/or pedal mount to allow full pushrod travel. Wilwood recommends using an adjustable proportioning valve to set the front to rear brake bias. See chapter 7 for inspection and testing procedures.

Master Cylinder Installation *Continued*

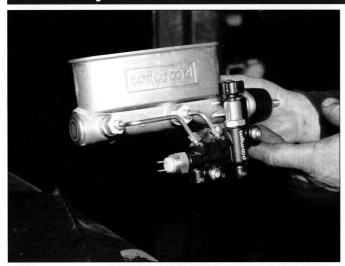

4 Wilwood supplies a combination valve that has an adjustable proportioning valve as well as a warning light sensor. Lines are pre-bent for an easy mount to the master cylinder. The combination valve does the job of three different components: a metering valve, a pressure differential switch, and a proportioning valve.

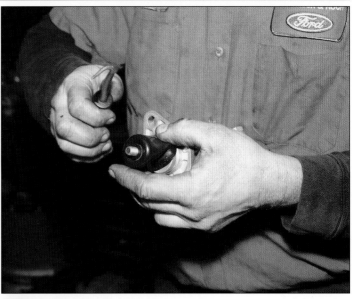

5 Before mounting the new master cylinder, be sure to install the rubber seal over the pushrod area. In this case, the factory pushrod and its position on the brake pedal were retained. This may be different in other applications.

6 Align the new tandem master cylinder with the brake booster mounting holes on the firewall and check all the lines for clearance.

7 With the master cylinder and the combination valve assembled, test fit it one more time then secure it in place. An assistant is needed to be inside to hold the retaining bolts. All lines and brake components should be double-checked for clearance of parts, such as exhaust manifolds, the exhaust system, or moving parts. Secure the assembly with the mounting bolts.

8 Once the master cylinder has been installed and the brake line correctly connected to the master cylinder, it's time to add brake fluid. Fill the master cylinder up to the full line with brake fluid. Wilwood recommends hand bleeding the master cylinder on the bench before installing it. With a power bleeder available, we bled it on the car.

9 To aid in the bleeding process, a handheld vacuum pump and reservoir were called in to assist. This helps the process, but final bleeding was done traditionally with the aid of an assistant and the call out: "Pump it. Hold it . . . and Release."

10 When bleeding is complete, top off with brake fluid and install the master cylinder cover. Unlike the factory cover with the spring retainer, the Wilwood cover is retained by four assembly screws.

11 Install the wheels, check for any interference and tools left lying on the lift or hidden away in any holding spots, then tighten the lug nuts to the proper torque spec.

MOPAR BRAKE CONVERSION: PRO TOURING UPGRADE

Much like General Motors and Ford Motor Company, the Chrysler Corporation didn't change the front suspension much on its intermediate and full-size cars and was able to use many of the common parts for several models in an effort to cut expenses. This situation has opened many options for enthusiasts of vintage Mopars, including using later-model disc brake systems on classic muscle cars.

Falling into this category are the intermediate cars made by Chrysler, Dodge, and Plymouth from 1962 to 1979. They are often referred to as B-Body after the platform used as

the base for these vehicles. However, many of these conversions will work on the smaller A-Body platforms, such as the Dart, Demon, Duster, and Valiant. The larger E-Body platforms, such as the later Barracuda and Challengers, also fall into this conversation.

In this chapter, we will take a look at some disc brake interchanges in the Chrysler family, including some mixing of parts from later-model Chrysler models to classic 1960s intermediate cars. Then we will look at a basic disc brake upgrade on a 1969 Dodge Dart, using a four-piston caliper front and rear set from Baer

Brakes. This project car was used as a research and development vehicle for the manufacturer to design and develop a complete brake kit for this model year Dodge.

As we detailed in chapter 1, Chrysler offered a disc brake system on the Crown Imperial limousine in 1949. The company continued with other models in 1950 as a $400 option. Very few of these were sold, and by 1954, Chrysler gave up on the disc brake option. The company would not offer another model with disc brakes until 1965. The Chrysler Company clearly had its target set on the muscle car market in the 1960s.

Chrysler engineers succeeded in taking their share by creating performance cars that people wanted to buy. The Charger and Road Runner were sales leaders and both

Chrysler's version of the pony car was built on the A-platform, commonly called A-Body cars. Pony cars have been the traditional base for modern Pro Touring–style builds. This chapter features a Dodge Dart Pro Touring–style brake upgrade with Baer Brakes.

This particular Mopar disc brake upgrade is part of a 1969 Dodge Dart research and development car for Baer Brakes. The upgrade consisted of a base disc brake front and rear kit from Baer that can be used for practically any application and can be upgraded with other Baer Brake systems later.

Our upgrade will replace the A-Body Kelsey-Hayes four-piston calipers with the popular Baer Brakes SS4+ four-piston calipers. Baer's SS4+ calipers offer more braking power in a more compact and lighter caliper than the stock-style cast calipers. This gives enthusiasts an option to upgrade braking and still use the popular stock-style 15-inch steel wheels.

became NASCAR game changers with advanced aerodynamic designs and horsepower. The Charger dominated on NASCAR's ovals for four years before the other manufacturers caught up. For consumers, the Dodge cars offered everything from economy street cars to the race-ready Hemi V-8 Sports Coupe.

Chrysler's Muscle Car Brake Systems

Chrysler used three different disc brake systems during the muscle car era. Model size and weight dictated which brake system was used in each of the platforms. The A-Body cars employed Kelsey-Hayes four-piston calipers with 11.04-inch rotors with cooling vents. The gray iron rotors were fitted with five 7/16-inch wheel studs in a 5x4-inch bolt circle pattern. The calipers were two-piece housings that were held together by two cap screw bridge bolts.

The four pistons were 1.64-inch (41.53-mm) outside diameter (OD). Fluid was transferred between the two halves by a short steel crossover tube. Replacement OEM-style calipers are still being produced by various manufacturers. This brake system was the standard on 1965–1969 Plymouth Barracuda, 1965–1972 Dodge Dart, and the 1965–1972 Plymouth Valiant.

Chrysler's intermediate-size vehicles on the B-platform used a Bendix caliper with four phenolic/aluminum 2-inch OD pistons. The Bendix calipers were similar in design to the Kelsey-Hayes calipers. The rotors were a larger $11^{1}/_{4}$ inch, fitted with 1/2-inch wheel studs in a 5x4.5-inch bolt circle pattern.

This system was common on the 1966–1969 Dodge Charger, 1966–1969 Dodge Coronet, 1966–1969 Plymouth Belvedere, 1966–1969 Plymouth Satellite, 1967–1969 Dodge Super Bee, R/T, GTX, and 1967–1969 Plymouth

Road Runner. This brake system was only slightly larger than the system used on the A-platform cars. Given the weight of these midsize Chrysler cars and the huge horsepower engines, this brake system was truly inadequate for these vehicles.

The full-size Chrysler C-platform cars used a four-piston caliper manufactured by the Budd Company. Not as well-known as Kelsey-Hayes or Bendix today, Budd was a metal fabricator and a major supplier of body components to the automobile industry from 1912 until its bankruptcy in 2014. In 1965, Budd was hired to design and manufacture a front disc brake system for Chrysler Corporation's line of full-size automobiles. This system was carried on through the 1968 model year.

The Budd-designed brake system was used on 1965–1968 full-size Chryslers: Plymouth Fury, Dodge Polara, Dodge Monaco, Custom 880, and 1967–1969 Chrysler Imperial nameplates. This system featured an

The Budd Company brake components for full-size Chrysler cars are very rare today and seldom seen. Thanks to the aftermarket industry, reproduction parts can often be found for enthusiasts who want to keep the stock-style system. (Photo Courtesy Stainless Steel Brakes Corporation)

11.88-inch vented rotor with a unique four-piston caliper. The system changed in 1969 with a slightly smaller 11.75-inch disc and remained that size for C-platform cars until their production was discontinued.

The only difference during the last production run from 1969 to 1972 was bearing size because the later hubs incorporated smaller wheel bearings. The hubs were all fitted with the 5x4.5-inch bolt circle pattern for the wheel studs. These calipers and rotors are very rare today and seldom seen. Stainless Steel Brakes Corporation has reproduced a single-piece rotor and hub

(part number 23077AA1A) for those enthusiasts wanting to restore these brake systems to stock-like condition.

There are very few aftermarket parts manufacturers that supply OEM-style brake parts for these full-size cars. Because Chrysler farmed out all of its brake manufacturing to outside vendors, the best opportunity to find original pieces is through wrecking yards.

The A- and B-platform cars are well serviced by the aftermarket parts suppliers. Because Kelsey-Hayes and Bendix were more prolific in the brake manufacturing industry, there are more opportunities for parts

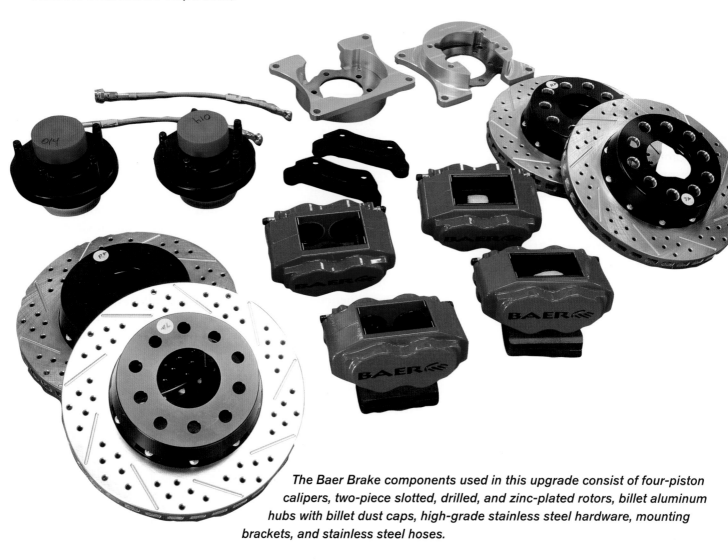

The Baer Brake components used in this upgrade consist of four-piston calipers, two-piece slotted, drilled, and zinc-plated rotors, billet aluminum hubs with billet dust caps, high-grade stainless steel hardware, mounting brackets, and stainless steel hoses.

cross-referencing. For example, the Kelsey-Hayes brake system used on the Chrysler A-platform cars was previously used on Ford Mustangs through 1967. The Bendix brake system used on Chrysler's B-platform cars was shared on several 1967–1969 Buick models and almost all of the 1965–1970 AMC vehicles.

While the Chrysler four-piston caliper brakes were decent performers for that time, they were not as resistant to brake fade on these heavier cars. As with most of the brake systems that were used 50 years ago, the OEM brakes do not compare with the modern brake technology and pose a safety issue. Even a simple swap to a modern budget-type disc brake system is a major upgrade and will keep you stopping safely for years to come.

The Baer Brakes Upgrade

Baer Brakes was born out of the movement for larger brakes on higher-horsepower Detroit muscle cars racing on road courses. This gave way to the Pro Touring breed of cars with low-profile tires on larger wheels with bigger brakes. This is where Baer Brakes emerged as a leader in the aftermarket brake industry.

While cast calipers certainly have their spot in the marketplace and fit into many project car budgets, they may not always fit into the Pro Touring car builds. This style of car build has been typically based on classic muscle cars with enhanced suspension components and drivetrain. These cars are built with an emphasis on function and are intended to be driven robustly or in competition. In this case, a big brake kit (BBK) is a better choice.

For this upgrade, Baer's SS4+ calipers were chosen for their four-piston clamping power in a smaller package to retain a factory-type 15-inch wheel. Baer's S4 calipers are a workhorse in the Baer lineup, finding use on just about every application imaginable.

The caliper's smaller size belies the fact that these calipers have all the benefits and clamping power of a larger brake system, which is perfect for an entry-level Pro Touring brake system. We were not concerned with a parking brake, so the SS4+ caliper was also a great fit on the rear to cosmetically match the front brakes.

Baer's SS4 and SS4+ calipers feature a two-piece billet aluminum housing that is held together with four cross bolts that strengthen the entire unit. Baer offers these calipers in a variety of color choices.

Baer offers a parking brake option in its Extreme+ and Pro+ brake kits for enthusiasts desiring parking brakes on its street-driven cars.

The SS4+ calipers are a two-piece billet aluminum construction made in Phoenix, Arizona, for those who support American-made products. The two halves are held together with four cross bolts to increase the stiffness of the caliper. The four pistons are hard anodized with stainless abutments to prevent wear and provide support. Baer's two-piece directionally vaned rotors are 11-inch slotted and drilled and zinc-plated. These were selected as the perfect match to the SS4+ calipers.

The front billet aluminum hubs are assembled at the factory with bearings and hand-packed with Red Line synthetic grease. The unit is topped with a billet dust cap. The rear brake system employs Baer's unique backing plate that not only acts as a caliper mount but also is the bearing retainer for the rear axle. This particular unit does not have a parking brake.

Removal and Inspection

We were in luck because our project car was outfitted with front disc brakes to begin with. This makes the conversion much easier. When changing from front drums to disc brakes on Chrysler muscle cars, the spindle will need to be changed. The drum spindle was made to hold the drum brake backing plate and will not mount or locate the disc brake caliper properly. Before starting, confirm that the correct spindle is used or source a new factory-style disc brake spindle.

As with any installation, take a careful inventory of the parts to make sure that everything required is accounted for before starting the removal. We've all had a project that has sat unfinished awaiting parts. If this happens to a daily driver, it could pose a problem. After a reasonable parts inspection is completed, the removal of the old components can begin. This project was not ordered as a kit, so our technicians thought through the installation and acquired all the parts that would theoretically complete the job based on similar installations.

Our crew began by loosening the brake lines at the frame using a 3/8-inch line wrench made for loosening brake line flair nuts. Use care to capture the brake fluid in the lines and cap the line at the frame to prevent any contamination from entering the line. A good assortment of vinyl line caps is a must for any serious mechanic doing brake systems.

With the brake line to the frame disconnected, remove the spring clip that holds the brake hose to the bracket. A pair of pliers or channel locks works well to remove these clips. The hose is free on the frame end and is still connected to the caliper on the other end. The caliper can be removed by loosening the two mounting bolts, then sliding the caliper off of the rotor with the hose attached.

Remove the hub by removing the spindle nut and pulling the hub and rotor off of the spindle. Normally, the spindle would be checked for damage and the bearing surfaces wrapped to prevent any scuffing or scratches on the spindle snout. Since we are replacing the spindle with a new factory-style spindle, it was left unprotected.

The backing plate and spindle can be removed together. The spindle is connected on the upper end by the upper ball joint in the upper control arm. On the bottom end, the spindle is supported by the steering arm, which also houses the lower ball joint. Remove the retaining nut

The factory-style disc brake spindles will mount on either side, but the location of the caliper dictates on which side the spindle will be installed. The calipers are designed to be on the leading or forward side of the rotor. This means the caliper is ahead of the axle centerline. For this upgrade, the calipers need to be moved to the trailing side, which means the spindles get mounted on the opposite side. On our research and development car, the calipers had already been relocated through a previous upgrade somewhere in its life.

The stock Kelsey-Hanes factory disc brake system on the A-platform cars performed admirably. For our purposes, we decided to remove the entire front brake system and replace it with an upgraded four-piston system from Baer Brakes that would allow us to keep 15-inch "steelies" on the car.

from the upper ball joint and use a ball joint separator to free the spindle on the top end. Remove the two steering knuckle mount bolts from the spindle and the spindle will be free from the front end. Clean and check the upper and lower ball joints and replace them if wear is apparent. Replacing the ball joints now prevents another maintenance cycle somewhere down the road, so consider it cheap insurance to replace them now.

The hubs used in this upgrade are designed for use with OEM-style B- and E-platform Mopar disc spindles from the 1973–1974 model years. Because the spindles are smaller in height, the factory control arms and ball joints for B- and E-platform cars will need to be used to make this upgrade work properly. These hubs are the same parts that Baer Brakes uses in the 1973–1974 Dodge Challenger/Plymouth Barracuda/Plymouth Satellite, 1973–1975 Dodge Charger/Dodge Coronet/Dodge Dart/Plymouth Duster/ and Plymouth Road Runner.

The upper control arm is removed by unbolting it at the cam bolts. The upper control arm can be pulled out and removed from the vehicle. It pays to bag and tag the hardware so that it can be used to identify the cam bolts and washer stack for installation. The bolts can be replaced or reused if they are in good shape.

New or reconditioned factory-style control arms and ball joints for B- and E-platform cars need to be sourced for this upgrade. If the parts are used from a recycling facility or wrecking yard, it would probably be wise to have the arms sandblasted and powder coated or painted. Carefully check the control arm bushings

The installation of the new brake system begins with the removal of the stock parts. This photo shows the dust cover removed and our technician removing the spindle nut to free the front hub for removal. Once the hub is removed, there is complete access to the spindle and backing plate.

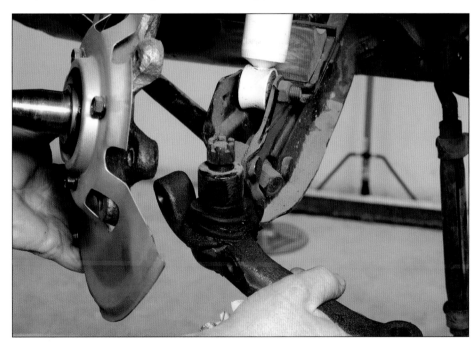

The spindle and backing plate are removed, showing the steering arm and lower ball joint. The spindle is the key to any brake system swap on Chrysler cars from this era. Most Mopar enthusiasts are familiar with the big bearing spindles that were only offered on the 1973 to 1976 A-platform cars. Those factory spindles are popular in home-garage disc brake conversions.

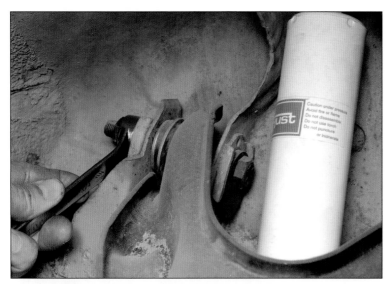

Upper control arms are mounted to the chassis by cam bolts that allow camber adjustment for the suspension. Swapping out these control arms means a front end alignment is needed immediately after the upgrade is completed, and it should not be skipped. Check the cam bolts and replace them if needed.

Using the shorter spindle requires using the corresponding upper control arm to keep the steering geometry correct. Using the factory-style B- and E-Body disc brake spindles with the 1973–1974 factory upper control arms and ball joints is a smart choice.

The lower ball joint is screwed into the steering arm and then bolted to the spindle. The steering arm can be installed on the spindle with common hand tools. For safety, a Chrysler ball joint socket should be used to remove and install the ball joints.

This photograph shows the components that were removed for the upgrade: the factory front disc brake system along with the stock 1969 Dart spindle, upper control arm, disc rotor, and backing plate. These parts can return money by selling the components on eBay or Craigslist to enthusiasts seeking stock components for a complete restoration project.

and replace them if necessary. Using new ball joints for the upper and lower control arms is also money well spent in the conversion.

Chrysler upper ball joints are threaded and require a special socket to remove and install the ball joints properly. It may be tempting to use a large adjustable wrench or a large 3/4-inch drive socket to remove or install the ball joint, but neither of these work as well as the special tool designed for that purpose.

In many cases, these can be rented or borrowed from your local auto supply parts store. Online parts suppliers, such as Jegs and Summit Racing, sell the Chrysler ball joint socket, and with shipping, the cost is somewhere around $50. Lower ball joints are threaded into the steering arms. The steering arms are bolted to the spindle and can be installed with common hand tools.

Taking the time to clean the inner fender well and suspension area where the new parts will mount is a real professional move. Vacuum out all of the debris, road grime, and dirt. Having a clean area to work serves many purposes. Not only will any problem areas be easier to see and inspection of the completed brake system upgrade easier to perform but also keeping crud from getting into eyes or other places is lessened. It is well worth the effort and time to take these steps, and it makes a better-looking project when it is completed.

Front Brake System Assembly

The installation can truly start by installing the spindles and upper control arms. The spindles included in this upgrade kit are reproduction Mopar B- and E-platform spindles from 1973–1974 as discussed earlier. The matching upper control arm and new ball joint must be installed to the chassis prior to bolting in the new spindle.

The Chrysler platforms came with calipers mounted to the leading side of the rotor. That is, the calipers were ahead of the axle centerline or spindle pin. The pins on these spindles have a larger outside diameter pad for the wheel bearings. The Baer Brakes billet hubs account for these larger wheel bearings.

The Baer Brakes instructions call for mounting the right-side spindles on the left side and the left-side spindles on the right side. This relocates the caliper to the aft side of the rotor, behind the axle centerline. There are many reasons why car manufacturers and aftermarket suspension or brake kit suppliers place the brake calipers in the front or back of the rotor.

Baer Brakes does this mainly for cosmetic reasons in this application. Moving the spindles from one side to the other only relocates the caliper position but will not alter the geometry of the suspension. Reattach the steering arm to the spindle with the original bolts and nuts. Torque the bolts to 160 ft-lbs.

The upper control arm, ball joint, and spindle are installed with the caliper mount located to the rear of the vehicle. The location of the caliper is done for clearance or personal preference. Most of Baer's customers prefer the rear mounted calipers for cosmetic reasons.

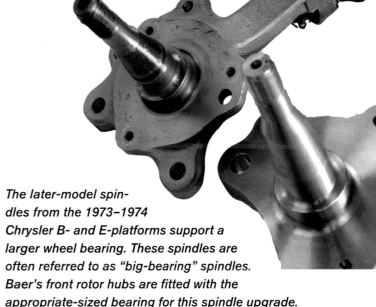

The later-model spindles from the 1973–1974 Chrysler B- and E-platforms support a larger wheel bearing. These spindles are often referred to as "big-bearing" spindles. Baer's front rotor hubs are fitted with the appropriate-sized bearing for this spindle upgrade.

Caliper Location

The location of disc brake calipers is determined by many different factors. Some are placed toward the front of the brake rotor; others are placed toward the rear. The factors that influence disc brake caliper location include suspension geometry and component clearance.

In some vehicles, disc brakes are cooled by air ducts and brake caliper placement can affect the airflow and cooling properties. Sports cars that have low ground clearance and rely on aerodynamics for speed and stability can be affected by caliper location. The purpose of the vehicle, cost, and cosmetics are all taken into consideration.

Many times, the location of disc brake calipers is centered around weight distribution. Stock brake calipers weigh from 3 to 5 pounds each. Mounting the front calipers behind the axle centerline and mounting the rear calipers in front of the rear axle centerline results in moving the weight of the calipers toward the center of the vehicle.

For several decades, one of the most common practices for caliper location on front rotors was the location of the steering rack. Automotive engineers designed the front calipers to be located on the opposite side of the steering rack. In moving the steering rack to the front of the car, the calipers were forced to the rear of the rotors for clearance, which also put the weight toward the car's center.

However, the most significant factor in caliper location boils down to suspension geometry and clearance of suspension components. For most daily driver street vehicles, the best location for disc brake calipers is simply the spot that is available after the rest of the suspension has been engineered. ■

Engineers place the caliper on the rotor at different points for various reasons. Many times, weight placement has a large impact on where the caliper is located. Lower is better for a low center of gravity. Toward the center of the car helps with balance. A caliper placed toward the rear affects the cooling air to the rotor less. In our case, placing the caliper to the rear was simply for looks.

The spindles are made with caliper mounting bosses inherent as a part of the spindle. As with many of the aftermarket brake systems, the rotors in the brake kits are larger, some very large. The difference in rotor size requires an intermediate bracket that locates the calipers at the proper distance and centers the caliper on the rotor.

These intermediate brackets are unique to the rotor diameter and rotor width. After the upper control arm and spindle are mounted to the suspension, the intermediate bar is attached to allow for the mounting of the caliper.

Baer brakes includes $1^1/_2$-inch long, 1/2-inch hex bolts with washers for mounting the intermediate bracket to the spindles. The bracket will need to be test fit to the spindle to ensure a tight and flush fit to the spindle. Most spindles are cast units with a slight variance in the outside surface of the spindles, particularly at the parting lines of the spindles. In some cases, the spindle will need to be ground down to allow the intermediate bracket to fit properly. The bracket is intended to be mounted with the part numbers facing inboard to the vehicle.

Test fit the bracket and remove material from the spindle as needed to allow clearance around the bolt

In order to mount the caliper, an intermediate bracket that locates the caliper on the rotor at the correct distance and has the correctly spaced mounting holes for attaching the caliper is included in the kit. This intermediate bracket must be test fit on the spindle for a flush fit.

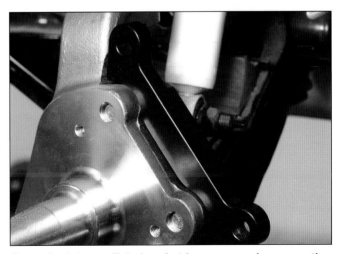

Due to the wide range of variance in spindle manufacturing, some material may need to be removed to allow the intermediate bracket to mount properly. Grind away enough material that the bracket has proper clearance.

Once the intermediate bracket has proper clearance, the mounting bolts and washers can be installed to secure the caliper in place. Tighten the bolts snugly for the purposes of shimming the calipers for exact placement on the rotor only.

mounting bosses to line up with the mounting holes on the spindle. The material removed from the spindle is such a small amount that it will not affect the strength of the spindle.

At this point in the installation, the intermediate bracket bolts are temporarily installed with a snug fit, as these will need to be shimmed to center the calipers on the rotors after the calipers are installed.

Baer's billet aluminum hubs are machined from 6061-T6 aluminum and come preassembled with bearings, races, and studs, and are packed with synthetic grease. Installation of the hub assembly on the spindle begins with applying a small amount of grease to the hub seal surface, then sliding the hub onto the spindle pin.

Place the outer bearing, washer, and spindle nut on the spindle pin to retain the hub assembly. The spindle nut should be tightened between 5 and 10 ft-lbs while the hub is slowly being spun to help seat the wheel bearings. The spindle nut should be loosened and retightened while spinning the hub several more times to ensure the bearings are fully seated.

Finally, the nut is tightened enough to remove axial play. Then, it is tightened approximately 1/16 of a turn or slightly more to align the cotter pin holes in the spindle with the slots in the castellated nut. This extra turn in the spindle nuts acts as a small preload for the bearings. After the cotter pin is inserted and the ends are bent to prevent the cotter pin from falling out, install the dust cap. The socket head bolts that retain the dust cap are torqued to 2 ft-lbs to complete the hub installation.

Next, install the correct-side rotor onto the hub and secure it in place using at least three lug nuts with washers to prevent scratching the rotor hat. When installing Baer rotors, follow the direction of rotation indicated on the rotor hat area with either an arrow or an "L" for left, an "R" for right, or both. "L" (left) always indicates the driver's side of vehicles. Ensure the brake pads are removed from the caliper, then install the caliper on either side; the right and left are identical (the SS4 calipers are manufactured with dual bleeders to allow installation on either side). The calipers will bolt to the intermediate bracket with M12-1.75x35-mm bolts and washers. Because the calipers will need to be shimmed to fit correctly, the bolts need only be tightened snugly for now.

The billet aluminum rotor hub, outfitted with wheel bearings and packed with synthetic grease, is inserted on the spindle pin. The retaining washer and spindle nut are threaded on the spindle pin threads. The spindle nut is tightened to seat the bearings, then loosened and retightened a couple of times to make sure the bearings are seated, then torqued while rotating the hub.

After torquing to the proper torque value, tighten the nut to line up the cotter pin holes to the grooves in the castle nut. Insert the cotter pin to prevent the nut from loosening, then install a dust cap to prevent contamination of the bearing grease.

Install the rotor onto the hub, making sure the correct side is installed. The rotor will be labeled with an L or R indicating the left or right side. The side of a vehicle is always determined from the perspective of sitting in the driver's seat. This makes the driver's side the left side, and the passenger's side on the right. Secure the rotor temporarily with lug nuts.

The shimming process is a method of measuring the gap between the caliper and rotor in four places, shimming the caliper until the gap is equal across the four measurements. Shimming the caliper to ensure complete clamping power and optimal wear characteristics must be performed. It is not enough to eyeball the distance between the caliper and rotor at all four points. Precision measuring equipment and a good procedure is needed. Baer's instructions with the brake kit explain that gap measurement from the caliper body to the rotor should be performed with a dial or a digital caliper.

Determining Caliper Shim Size

1. Using a vernier caliper, measure the gap from the rotor to the caliper body at four points: top inside, top outside, bottom inside, and bottom outside. Write these measurements down.

2. Subtract the top inside measurement from the top outside measurement. Half of the difference between the two measurements is the size of the shim for the top bracket bolt. For example, if the top inside measurement is 0.865 inch, and the top outside measurement is 0.905 inch, that is a difference of 0.040 inch. Half of that difference is 0.020 inch, which is the size of shim required for the top bracket.

3. Do the same for the bottom measurements to determine the shim size of the intermediate bracket mount. Getting these gaps as close as possible within 0.005 inch will keep the possibility of excessive noise to a minimum.

   Note: There may be different-sized shims required for the top and bottom. The need for shimming is due to the variations in spindle manufacturing and wear at the bearing seat area at the inner bearing. ■

Remove the brake pads from the caliper, and slide the caliper onto the rotor, and secure the caliper with the caliper mounting bolts.

Shimming Procedure

After determining the correct shim sizes, remove the caliper and loosen the intermediate bracket bolts. Insert the correctly sized shim between the bracket and the spindle. This is best accomplished by removing one bolt at a time, inserting the shim, reinstalling the bolt, and tightening it snugly for a check of the fitment. Reinstall the caliper and recheck the gap measurement. Then, reshim if it is necessary.

Continue this process until the top and bottom gap measurement is within 0.005 inch. Once the shimming process is completed, install the brake pads. Then, torque the bracket bolts to 95 ft-lbs and the caliper bolts to 85 ft-lbs.

Finger tighten the steel-braided hose with the banjo hose end into the inside of the caliper with one copper washer on each side of the banjo fitting. Then, connect the steel-braided hose to the hard line at the frame and install the hose lock to secure the hose. Have an assistant turn the steering wheel through the full range and watch to ensure the hose is positioned so that it doesn't interfere with any suspension or steering components. Finish by torquing the banjo bolt from 15 to 20 ft-lbs. Repeat these steps for the other side and recheck the lines and bolts for security.

The shims are washers of various thickness that are used to move the caliper's distance in relationship to the rotor. Once the gap is equal, tighten and torque the bolts for security.

To finalize the conversion, the supplied steel-braided brake lines are installed. The banjo fitting is connected to the caliper with a special banjo bolt and two copper washers for sealing. The other end of the hose attaches to the hard line on the frame.

The Rear Brake System

For the rear brake system, we selected Baer's 11-inch Rear SS4+ Brake System No Park Brake. Like the front brake system, the rear kit features the SS4+ calipers mounted to an 11-inch, two-piece, slotted, drilled, and zinc-plated rotor. The rotors come preassembled with high-grade stainless hardware. The real key to this kit is Baer's unique backing plate that acts as both a caliper mount and a bearing retainer. The kit was designed as a general fit for Dana 60/8.75-inch rear axle with an axle flange diameter of 5.9 inches or less. The kit includes the stainless braided hoses and fits most 15-inch and larger wheels.

Many Dodge models came factory-equipped with a Dana 60 or 8.75-inch rear end. These have served many automatic transmission big-block Super Bees, Road Runners, and even the famous Daytona aero-cars. This kit is designed specifically for the Dana 60/8.75-inch rear ends.

With the vehicle safely supported and the wheels off the ground, the disassembly of the stock brake system can be started. Almost everything needed is in the Baer Brakes kit, but the gasket between the backing plate and the rear end housing may need to be replaced. It would be smart to order two of these gaskets (one for each side) before starting the rear end brake upgrade.

Begin by removing bolts on the bearing retainer that hold the axle

The Baer Brakes 11-inch Rear SS4+ Brake System has no provision for a parking brake. Many other Baer Brakes kits include provisions for a parking brake. The key components in this system are the same SS4+ brake calipers and 11-inch rotors as the front brake system. The axle bearing retainer/ rotor hat is the real key to this kit.

Many of the Mopar models used either Dana 60 or 8.75-inch rear ends as their rear suspension platform. The Baer Brakes kit is tailor-made for these rear ends, providing a new level of braking performance that was not available when these rear ends were first released to the public. Almost all were fitted with drum brakes, as was the case with our research and development project car.

to the rear end housing. Remove the axle shaft. Take a good look at the shaft and make sure that it is still serviceable. Check the bearings and seal for wear and replace if necessary. If the axle is difficult to remove from the rear end housing, a slide hammer with hub puller attachment can be used to simplify the process.

Disconnect the brake fluid line from the slave cylinder on the backside of the backing plate. Use care to not kink or break the hard line when moving it away from the backing plate. This line will be reused with the new Baer Brakes rear disc brake system.

Remove the backing plate and disconnect the parking brake cable from the frame mount and remove the cable and backing plate from the vehicle.

The axle can be reinstalled now, taking care to slide the retainer over the studs on the housing. The origi-

The axle shafts are pulled by removing the bearing retainer plate and the bolts holding the retainer plate to the axle flange. The stock-style axles have an access hole that allows access to the bearing retainer plate bolts. This simplifies the job tremendously.

nal stock axles have an access hole for installing and tightening the bearing retainer nuts. Some aftermarket replacement stock-style axles may not have this access hole. A slim-line box wrench or other special tool may be used to tighten the retainer nuts. If there is an access hole in the axle face, install the retainer nuts and torque them to 45 ft-lbs.

After the axle has been pulled, the parking brake cable should be removed from the backing plate, and the backing plate can be removed without having to disassemble the brake shoe assembly. These parts can be cleaned and also sold on eBay or Craigslist to an enthusiast looking for OEM factory-style parts.

The Baer Brakes two-piece axle bearing retainer and rotor hat assembly is fitted to the axle flange after the axle has been reinstalled. The rotor hat fits on the flange first, followed by the axle, then the bearing retainer is attached. The rotor hat is secured with the bearing retainer nuts.

Use the access hole in the face of the axle shaft to tighten and torque the axle retaining nuts. Without this access hole, the ability to tighten the nuts is restricted. When replacing the axle shafts, it pays to find an aftermarket axle with the access hole. There are many on the market that do not.

Caliper and Bracket Installation

The SS4+ caliper will locate behind the axle centerline, just like the front brake system. Baer Brakes does this based on customer feedback. Most installers and builders prefer the calipers placed behind the axle centerline based on cosmetics. Start by attaching the radial mount bracket using the 12-mm non-Vibra-Tite bolts included in the kit. These can be tightened snugly using a 12-mm wrench. The rotor should be installed next, using at least three lug nuts with washers to prevent marring the rotor hat's finish.

With the brake pads removed, install the caliper with washers, retaining nuts, and mounting bolts. The bolts can be either 12-point black bolts or 12-mm Allen-head bolts. Just snug the bolts down so the calipers can be measured for caliper alignment by following the same shimming procedures outlined in the caliper shimming sidebar.

Once the shimming procedure is completed, install the brake pads in the caliper and install them over the rotor. Reinstall the washers, caliper retaining nuts, and caliper bolts. Torque these mounting bolts to 85 ft-lbs to secure the caliper in place.

The steel-braided hose with the banjo end fitting is installed in the caliper using the banjo bolt and copper washers that are also supplied in the kit. One copper washer goes on each side of the banjo fitting with the bolt securing the banjo fitting to the caliper.

Before tightening the banjo bolt, install the other end of the steel-braided line to the chassis hard line at the frame and install the hose lock. Torque the braided line fitting to the hard line fitting between 15

Install the rotor on the axle hub with three lug nuts to hold the rotor in place and flush against the hub. The caliper (without brake pads) can then be bolted to the caliper mount for alignment. The shimming procedure is the same as the front caliper alignment.

Shim the rear caliper, then torque the caliper mount bolts to secure the caliper to the mount. Take the time to check all the hardware for security and tightness.

and 20 ft-lbs. Use care to ensure the hose is positioned to avoid any interference with the wheel or suspension components through the entire range of motion.

Finally, torque the banjo bolt between 15 and 20 ft-lbs. Repeat this operation for the other side of the rear end and finalize the installation by rechecking all the fitting connections and bolts.

Don't Forget the Master Cylinder

We've covered the front and rear disc brake system upgrade for a Pro Touring or autocrossing Mopar platform with stock steel wheels, but a check of the master cylinder is needed for safety purposes. Baer Brakes will sell a remastered master cylinder for your upgrade if needed. If the brake system has a single-reservoir master cylinder, it should absolutely be replaced with a split-reservoir master cylinder during a disc brake upgrade.

The experts at Baer recommend a 15/16-inch bore size master cylinder for manual brakes, 1-inch bore master cylinder for systems with a power brake booster, and the larger $1^{1}/_{8}$-inch bore for hydro-boost systems. The 15/16-inch bore can be used for power or manual systems depending on desired pedal feel.

The 15/16-inch bore with a power booster offers a softer pedal feel with less pedal effort for actuation. The 1-inch bore with power booster will work well as long as the engine has good vacuum numbers and the booster is working properly. Lastly, hydro-boost or drag racing applications with dual rear calipers should use the $1^{1}/_{8}$-inch bore remaster master cylinders.

Installation of a brake master cylinder is pretty straightforward: drain and remove the old master cylinder and replace it with a new one on the brake booster or firewall. Always follow the instructions provided with the master cylinder kit.

The Baer Brakes SS4+ calipers we installed were the standard Baer Brakes red, but these are also offered in 28 other colors ranging from Grabber Blue and Hugger Orange to a polished finish. We installed the slotted and drilled rotors with a zinc-plated finish in this upgrade. Baer also offers slotted-only (without zinc-plating) and plain rotor options.

Install the steel-braided brake line just like the front brake system. The banjo fitting and connection to the hard line at the frame are identical to the front caliper's brake line. Double-check the hose to make sure it is clear of any potential pinch points that could crush or puncture it.

Don't forget to check the master cylinder. A split-reservoir master cylinder is a must. Bore size is important for the pedal feel and actuation of the braking system. Our installation was on a manual brake system, so the stock master cylinder was retained.

The final step in any brake system installation is bleeding the brake system to eliminate any air bubbles. More information on the brake system bleeding process is in chapter 7.

PICKING A SYSTEM AND GETTING IT DONE

We've taken a brake upgrade tour through Detroit's Big Three muscle car offerings and compared a few different options from OEM-style parts interchanges to top-shelf aftermarket brake kits and everything in between. In this final chapter, a path is provided to help enthusiasts decide which type of brake system is right for any application by using a detailed process that covers determining the requirements and researching upgrade options.

Once the decision has been made, a plan to execute a build strategy must be developed. Finally, a guideline is provided for inspecting your upgraded brake system and breaking in the components for a long and safe operational life.

There are many parts of a brake system that must work together in order to stop a muscle car. As this cutaway shows, the ventilated rotor, caliper, bearings, parking brake, mounting brackets, and spindle all combine at the wheel to stop a vehicle. These are only a part of the complete brake system.

Brake kit options range from stock-like to purpose-built for specific applications. Choosing the right balance of calipers and rotors can be confusing. Understanding the options and the applications will help any enthusiast make the right choice. (Photo Courtesy Wilwood Engineering Inc.)

Deciding on Your Brake System

With an aftermarket full of options, narrowing them down to get the best brake upgrade for your application can be an exhaustive and difficult process. While it may seem like an arduous task, the perfect selection boils down to where you are starting from and where you plan to end up with your pride and joy. Other factors, such as a budget, personal preferences, maintenance, performance, and even driving habits can influence the decision. Weighing these factors in a practical manner will culminate in a selection that will bring satisfaction and enjoyment.

Performing brake upgrades can be handled by an enthusiast or sent out to a professional installer. Needless to say, hiring a second party to install the brake system will add to the cost, but it will likely shorten the time the vehicle is off the street, and the work will be done correctly.

The downside of hiring an installer is the additional research to pick a dependable shop that fits within your budget. Fortunately, most of the aftermarket brake kits are simple installations that can easily be performed by enthusiasts with basic maintenance experience.

The first step in deciding on a brake system for your muscle car is determining the requirements for your vehicle and the application. Cost will always be a factor, but the finances can be somewhat controlled by focusing on the actual needs of the vehicle to meet the goals. In other words; spend what you need without overkill.

The best way to achieve getting the biggest bang for the buck is to be honest with yourself about the over-

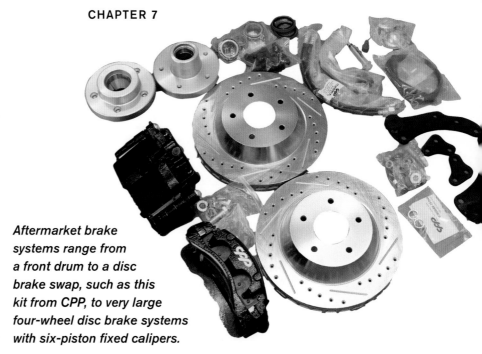

Aftermarket brake systems range from a front drum to a disc brake swap, such as this kit from CPP, to very large four-wheel disc brake systems with six-piston fixed calipers.

Category	Classification	Kits
Daily Driver		
	Stock disc upgrade	Front only, rear only, or both. Single-piston sliding caliper with a single-piece cast-iron rotor.
	Mild performance	Single-piece, increased-size, cast-iron rotor. Single-piston sliding caliper or two-piston fixed caliper.
	Weekend warrior	Street/strip, increased-size, single-piece rotor with aluminum calipers and billet aluminum mounting brackets.
Performance Upgrade		
	Autocrossing/Pro Touring	Medium to large two-piece steel rotors. Four- or six-piston aluminum fixed calipers.
	Drag racing	Forged one-piece slotted steel rotor. Directional calipers with staggered piston sizes.
	Road racing	Six-piston, billet aluminum, fixed calipers, large slotted rotors.
High Performance (Track Only)		
	Drag racing	Lightweight, single-caliper or dual-caliper system, two-piece slotted, floating rotors.
	Road racing	Upgraded materials, rotors, and pads. Fixed four- or six-piston calipers, two-piece slotted rotors.
	Circle track racing	Fixed four-piston calipers with two-piece steel rotors.

While the factory brakes were adequate for the time, modern materials and manufacturing procedures have advanced to the point where vintage technology is not as safe on today's highways. Knowing what is on the vehicle and what the future application for the car is will dictate the type of braking system that needs to be installed on a project car.

all objectives. Buying an eight-piston set of calipers with huge rotors to upgrade from a drum brake setup on your daily driver is probably not very cost effective. It will look spectacular and certainly generate some conversation at the next cars, coffee, and donuts meet, but it won't win you any awards driving to and from work.

The Daily Driver Category

For our purposes, breaking the goals down into three basic categories will help filter down the requirements. Let's start with the first category: daily driver. The typical daily driver muscle car will likely be a four-wheel drum brake car but may have factory disc brakes in the front. The car owner probably will be looking to upgrade to disc rotors for safety with some performance gains.

The initial decision with a daily driver conversion is whether the vehicle is going to upgrade the front brake system only, the rear brake system only, or both. These kits will probably consist of single-piston sliding calipers with solid 11- or 12-inch cast-iron rotors. Most of the kits in the entry-level or daily driver category offer disc brake upgrades that fit behind factory-style wheels as small as 15 inches. These kits still provide a substantial improvement in performance without necessitating a larger wheel and tire package, keeping the overall cost down.

The next step up in the daily driver class is a mild performance upgrade that goes beyond the single-piston basic disc brake caliper and 11-inch rotor. For enthusiasts who drive a little more spirited or tackle windy roads with gusto, a mild performance upgrade is warranted.

Keep in mind that larger rotors generally require larger wheels and sometimes suspension upgrades. This option should be thoroughly researched and planned before considering it a mild performance, budget upgrade. Kits in this range are probably a single sliding-piston caliper or a two-piston fixed caliper with a solid cast-iron rotor.

The third and final stage in the daily driver category is a street/strip weekend warrior build. For the

The brake system installed on the vehicle will have a direct impact on the wheel and tire package used. One current trend in daily drivers and street performers is a factory-style steel wheel. These are typically 15-inch wheels that require a compact but powerful brake caliper and rotor combination.

Two-pin sliding calipers were the popular OEM-type calipers due to their inexpensive manufacturing process, ease of maintenance, and reliability. These continue to be the common type of calipers on cars made at the factory. The simple sleeve and guide pin mechanism was the foundation for modern sliding calipers.

Entry-level street/strip performance kits, such as this Wilwood front brake kit, feature four-piston calipers that mount directly on a stock spindle. Forged billet hubs, steel rotors, and all the hardware provide a huge weight savings over stock brakes. Wilwood claims this kit saves 30 pounds over the stock brakes and fits inside 15-inch wheels, which makes it perfect for street/strip applications. (Photo Courtesy Wilwood Engineering Inc.)

Autocross has become a very popular motorsport with enthusiasts who want to use their daily driver in competition. An autocross course is basically a mini road course in a large parking lot or on unused airport tarmac, designed to see who can drive it the quickest without hitting any cones or going off course. These courses can be tough on brake systems.

enthusiast who has put some more grunt into his or her muscle car and challenges himself or herself and others at the local drag strip for bragging rights, a brake system made for mild street and strip performance should be considered. These systems would be on the higher end of the daily driver budget.

Stock brake systems are designed for street speeds and comfortable pedal feel. The more an enthusiast moves away from street-legal speeds and toward drag racing performance, selecting a brake system that optimizes that purpose will allow the vehicle to perform better. An entry-level street/strip brake system will combine budget with weight savings. These kits will feature one-piece steel rotors with lightweight aluminum calipers, and billet aluminum mounting brackets.

The Performance Category

The performance muscle car category consists of cars that are upgraded to the point where they are more performance-minded than personal commuter. The biggest performance upgrades are usually in the powertrain with likely suspension enhancements to help get power to the pavement.

At this stage, enthusiasts upgrade their muscle cars for a specific purpose. Autocrossing and Pro Touring applications demand higher-performance calipers and rotors that can withstand multiple hard applications of the brakes in a shorter timeframe. These systems will need to focus on resisting brake fade. Kits will probably have medium- to large-size, two-piece rotors with four- or six-piston aluminum calipers that require upgrading to 17- or 18-inch wheels.

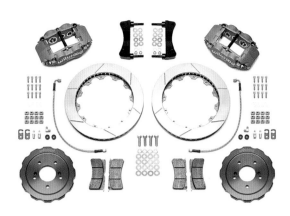

Wilwood's Forged Superlite 6R Big Brake Front Brake Kit is a great example of a big brake road race brake system. This kit features six-piston calipers matched with 12.88-inch directional vane rotors. These rotors are fitted to forged aluminum hats. Then radial mount brackets secure the fixed calipers to the OEM location without modification.

Today's big brake kits have larger rotors and multi-piston calipers that require more room than their factory counterparts. These larger rotors require a larger wheel and tire combination that will add to the overall cost of the brake system upgrade. The extra cost must be considered when evaluating a big brake kit.

High-performance brakes are purpose-built for very specific applications. When used in competition, these brakes are usually subject to technical inspections from sanctioning bodies or track officials at racing events. Competitive brake systems are considered important safety features of a race car, and rules are written to ensure a minimum standard is met.

The next class in the performance category is drag racing brakes, which focuses on braking power from higher speeds. Improved billet aluminum directional calipers with staggered pistons for even brake pad wear and less drag are available. Kits also include improved brake pad material, and two-piece steel rotors with aluminum rotor hats will increase the braking performance along with a speed performance through weight savings and drag reduction.

Some rotors in these kits are slotted. Slotted rotors allow for greater heat expansion and prevent the rotor from distorting.

Drag racing applications require a braking system that is lightweight but powerful enough to stop a higher-horsepower car at the end of the run. In many cases, drag cars will supplement the braking system with a parachute to help slow down the car.

Finally, the road race class of high-performance brakes places a high priority on clamping power and maximum braking over a longer period of time. Material selection is important in this class. Directional calipers with six pistons in a staggered design, better brake pad material, and improved forged rotors with aluminum rotor hats will be a substantial part of the road race upgrade kits in the performance category.

The Racing Category

The racing category is reserved for cars that are track-only race cars and don't see any action on the streets. Sanctioning-body rules should be followed in any competitive motorsport. However, if the rules allow the use different-style brake systems, choose one that will serve you best.

Drag racing brakes in this category are selected for high-powered cars that need to stop fast but not often. These may (but seldom do) include a second caliper on each rotor to increase the stopping power. Track-only drag brakes tend to have weight saving in mind. To accomplish this, the rotors are usually thinner with less material. This makes them suitable for single-purpose stops at the end of a drag strip run but not for everyday street driving.

Floating rotors are used to allow for radial and axial expansion.

Road racing brakes are also selected for high-powered engines that have to slow down more frequently and must stay cooler to ward off brake fade. These are commonly four- or six-piston calipers with two-piece rotors made from different metals. Rotor ventilation is greatly improved.

Many companies offer a two-piece lightweight rotor made from

Cooling vanes in the rotor help control the transfer of heat generated by the conversion of energy. The cross-drilled holes that help with the outgassing created by the brake pad material are drilled into the cooling vanes to help get rid of the gasses. This photo shows the relationship of the cross-drilled holes and cooling vanes.

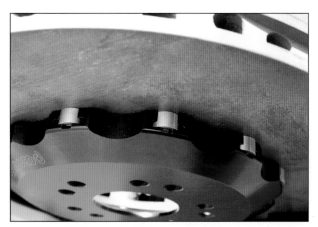

Higher-performance brake systems usually include two-piece rotors with each piece made of different materials for handling the heat transfer. The rotors may be floating-type rotors to allow for expansion, and the rotor width will likely be larger to accommodate larger ventilation vanes. Rotors subject to harsh treatment will probably be plain surface without cross-drilled holes or grooves to minimize the chance of cracking.

Road racing applications require a braking system that can handle a higher heat range due to the amount of braking on the track. Many times, these are larger brake kits that can transfer and dissipate the heat better to combat brake fade.

carbon ceramic material that is extremely resistant to heat buildup. The cost for these exotic conversion kits is a little higher than a street drum to disc conversion, but the brake system's stopping power remains strong even under the most grueling conditions.

Circle track brakes are a breed of their own with a heavy emphasis on brake pad material and rotors. There are differences between circle track brake systems based on the size of the track and the rules of the sanctioning body. Many of these rules attempt to keep a stock-like brake system. Smaller tracks require larger brake systems and external help with cooling to resist brake fade. Ducts and fans are often used in this class of brakes.

Front to rear caliper piston sizes, rotor diameters, and pad compounds will need to be configured to provide the correct brake bias when using a single bore master cylinder. Often, an inline adjustable proportioning valve is used to control the vehicle's brake balance.

Race applications often have systems that are not seen in street-legal vehicles. One of the most common race systems in road racing and circle track applications is a single-mount brake pedal with dual master cylinders and a balance bar to control and fine-tune the brake bias. In these race systems, the master cylinder size can be used to help control the car's brake balance. Larger-bore master cylinders will generate less pressure while decreasing pedal travel. Smaller-bore master cylinders will generate higher line pressures with an increase in pedal travel. Crews will change master cylinders as needed to suit the driver's preference or track conditions.

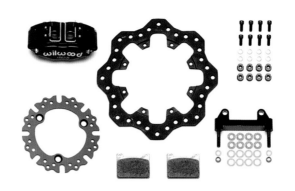

Circle track brake systems pose different concerns, especially those on dirt tracks. A system such as this front Dirt Modified brake kit address those concerns. For these racers, lightweight and low cost are the prime criteria for brake selection. Wilwood's Powerlite radial mount calipers and 11.75x0.35-inch scalloped lightweight rotors for the front tend to meet the needs of asphalt and dirt track modified racers.

Some competitive brake systems utilize a pedal system with two master cylinders that incorporate a balance bar that adjusts the brake bias from front to rear. The brake bias balance bar can be seen in this photo where the two master cylinder pushrods connect to the brake pedal.

Research Options

It is often difficult to know where to go to get the correct and most accurate information to research all the options available. Believe it or not, one of the best sources for advice is the tech line at each aftermarket manufacturer. These manufacturers work hard to build their brand. It is in their best interest to make sure customers get the right brake kit for their car or application. Unhappy consumers who send kits back and make comments on social media are not good for the company and might do irreparable harm. Companies have a reputation to maintain, and getting the right brake kit in the hands of the public is the best way to build a brand and help sales.

Use caution when researching on the internet. Many online magazines are supported by aftermarket manufacturers. Much like the print magazines of yesterday, the online magazines are advertiser based. Companies pay for advertising in the magazine. Magazine publishers will promote the products of their

It may not sound like much, but swapping from a stock-sized rotor disc to a big brake rotor disc can make a huge difference in braking potential. When stacked side-by-side, the difference is very noticeable.

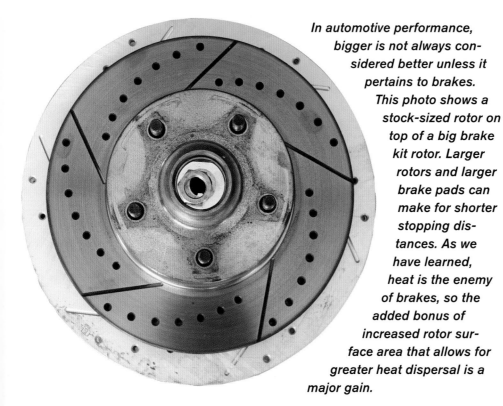

In automotive performance, bigger is not always considered better unless it pertains to brakes. This photo shows a stock-sized rotor on top of a big brake kit rotor. Larger rotors and larger brake pads can make for shorter stopping distances. As we have learned, heat is the enemy of brakes, so the added bonus of increased rotor surface area that allows for greater heat dispersal is a major gain.

advertisers over non-advertisers, and that is good marketing business sense for publications.

Just because you read it in a magazine does not mean it is the best or that the publisher even believes in the product. Usually, it means that the product is manufactured by an advertiser. The most accurate articles come from magazines that buy the products on the market and do a head-to-head comparison and review. These magazines most likely do not rely on advertising to support their work.

Keep in mind that the information superhighway can be the misinformation superhighway. Some online publications are very good, and some leave much to be desired. Use trusted sources when researching online.

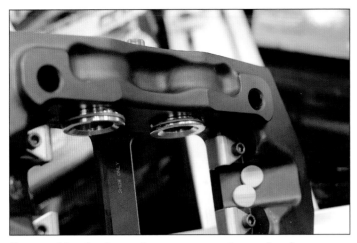

Researching brake system components can be done online through trusted websites, books on the subject, and by visiting larger car shows, such as the Goodguys or National Street Rod Association (NSRA) car shows, where vendors show their products. Notice the "Show Only" stamp on the caliper shown in the photo. These car shows are where you can go to physically touch and inspect the components to see the number of pistons, types of materials, and have any questions answered by technicians.

Knowing what you need and what you can afford can help you select the right brake system for your application. Considerations, such as wheel backspacing, rotor size, heat transfer, and other factors, must be weighed before investing in a brake system.

Print publications, such as this book, are vetted by the publisher and editor to a higher degree than internet publications and forums. It takes a lot of finances to actually put information into print, and the last thing a print publisher wants is a magazine or book that is inaccurate and no one wants to buy.

The information in these print publications is usually more scrutinized and verified before the text will ever hit the printing press. The goal with print books is to produce a written work that will be relevant for several years. Much like online publications, some print sources are very good and others may not be as good. Rely on those sources that are well respected and trusted in the community.

Developing and Executing a Build Strategy

Many different brake systems are on the aftermarket these days, which means many different choices are available. Choices and options result in a lot of ways to make mistakes.

The easiest way to prevent making a huge and costly mistake is to develop a build strategy. This is good advice, and not just for a selecting and building a brake system either. A construction plan that takes all the factors into account before spending a single dollar will help navigate the waters.

The largest obstacle to overcome is the difference between what you want and what you can afford. Practically anything is possible, providing you have an endless supply of money. There is a story that race car builders like to tell. A driver goes into a speed shop and asks, "How fast can you make a car go?" The shop owner answers that question with one of his own, "How much money do you have?" The same can be said of stopping: How much money do you have?

By now you probably have a good idea of what to do with your project car: enjoying the trip to and from work daily or competing with other enthusiasts at the track or on the windy road. Perhaps you will simply be taking your Restomod to the local car show and sharing it with other fans of vintage Detroit iron. Whatever your goal happens to be, the project starts with that goal, that single purpose.

1. Determine Your Goal.

Just picking out parts or a random kit may have all the parts for a brake system, but that doesn't mean

Aftermarket brake companies, such as Baer Brakes, specialize in offering enthusiasts a wide range of products from an OEM replacement upgrade to an elite racing spec brake system, such as this R-Spec iron race rotor and 6R caliper. While these top-of-the-line systems are impressive, they may not be what you need. These companies work to build an honest brand name and welcome your tech calls to ensure that enthusiasts get the system that best serves their needs.

Choosing a brake system to fit your needs may lead to a system with larger six-piston calipers, directional rotors, and brake pads with specific material. The cost for these types of systems is equal to the benefits provided by these systems. The brake system is one of those areas where you truly get what you pay for. Plan for this expense in your budget.

that it will do exactly what you want it to do. Picking out a system for Formula 1 road racing will work to slow down your door-slammer drag racer, but the cost may not be the most efficient.

Take a look around at your competition. See what kind of systems they are using. Talk to people who own the same type of car and are doing what you plan to do with the vehicle. You should have a good idea what you want your brake system to look like.

Picking the wrong brake system for your application can be costly. A mistake of that proportion can seriously dent your wallet. Any money spent to correct that kind of mistake will take away from spending money elsewhere on the car. This can keep you in the back of the pack, so it pays to do it right the first time. Figuring out what to do with your car will help with the next part of your build strategy.

2. Set a Budget.

Knowing what you want is one thing. Knowing what you can afford is something completely different. Set a budget. An honest budget. If you are planning to pay someone else to do the work, what do they charge? If you do the work, will you rent a garage or work out of your home garage? Do you need any tools? Will you rent or purchase these tools? If any parts go to be sandblasted or powder coated, this needs to be figured into the budget.

Almost every project build runs into a glitch and decisions need to be made to purchase an additional part or rebuild an old one. Adding a little cushion to your budget for this fudge factor will make things easier when the glitch comes up. Once you have a budget, do your best to stay in your planned budget. This will make the entire experience a pleasant one.

3. Acquire the Parts.

Once you have a budget, you should know what parts are needed. Research the options and do some comparison shopping. Use eBay to see what used systems will cost and how much it will take to restore the kit to like-new condition. Leave no stone unturned. Use message boards and clubs to find out where the best buys are. Then, purchase the parts in kit form whenever possible.

These kits are usually more complete and the home builder has a better chance to complete the project on schedule. Plus, the entire job tends to be less expensive when the parts are purchased together in kit form. Keep an inventory of the parts and don't begin the project until all the parts are acquired to do the job correctly.

If the brake system that was selected requires a larger tire and wheel package, make sure it is included in the plan. Call the brake company's tech line and ask which wheels have been tested with their kit. This will give you an idea where to start the search for a new set of wheels. (Photo Courtesy of Wilwood Engineering Inc.)

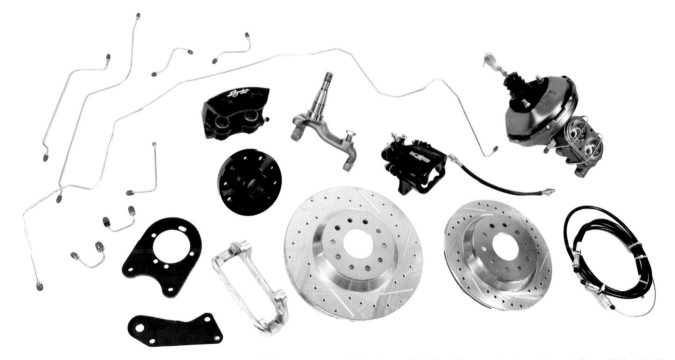

List the parts needed to complete the upgrade. Whenever possible, buy a kit that is complete and contains all the individual components. It is usually less expensive to get the parts in kit form, and it is less likely to have a key piece missing and have to make an emergency run to the parts store.

When the kits and parts arrive, take the time to read the instructions and make sure any parts that are required in the instructions are in the kit or purchased as needed. This includes tires and wheels if the brake kits require larger wheels.

4. Understand the Project.

Once the instructions have been read to ensure that all parts that will be needed are available, reread the instructions with an eye on the tasks. Again, be honest when assessing your skills. Not everyone is comfortable working on brake systems.

If there is a part of the job that you are not comfortable with, hire a professional to do that part of the job. If you can't bend or flare brake lines, contract it out to an expert who can do it quicker and cheaper. There's no harm in contracting work out. Enthu-siasts hire engine builders for their engine work all the time. The same is true of smaller projects. Don't be afraid to farm out difficult work.

5. Plan and Start the Job.

Where most people get in trouble is beginning the job with limited time. Starting and stopping a job numerous times increases the probability of mis-placing parts or skipping steps. Plan to start the job on a weekend when nothing else is planned.

Keep the parts close to the project. Any parts removed should be bagged and tagged, even if you don't plan on reusing them. You may want to sell the OEM brake system or keep it in case you ever want to take the vehicle back to stock. Having the parts bagged and tagged will help in either case.

If you have helpers, make sure that you supervise the job and keep track of the work being done and the parts being removed and installed. Use the instructions as a checklist or make your own checklist.

6. Inspect the Work.

Don't take anything for granted. Once the parts have been installed, go back to the instructions and physi-cally put a hand and eye on each part installed in sequence. Touch the bolts and nuts to make sure they are tight-ened and torqued.

Make sure the brake lines are connected properly and routed as to not interfere with the suspension or moving parts. Check for leaks after the system is filled with fluid and the system is bled. Brake fluid is very cor-rosive and catching any leaks is vital for public safety and protection of the vehicle.

7. Perform a Safety Check.

In addition to checking for loose or missing parts, perform a driving safety check before putting the vehi-cle in service. After a safety check is done, the brake pads and rotors should be broken in by the manufac-turer's recommendations.

Different brake pad and rotor materials require different bedding-in procedures. Make sure to follow the manufacturer's recommendations to ensure a longer life and safe opera-tion. If your kit's instructions do not include a safety inspection or the break-in procedures, we included generic procedures for both later in this chapter.

In planning the upgrade, don't forget to add in time for restoring any components that will be reused. In the case of a front disc upgrade where stock spindles are reused, plan on clean-ing and painting the stock spindle for a more professional look. Note that we used a bench vise with a bolt through the spindle's lower mount to hold it for cleaning and painting.

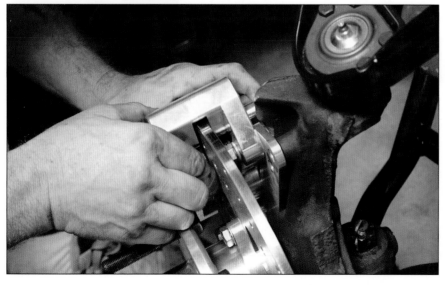

At the end of the installation, perform a full inspection of all components in the area where work was done. Physically touch each component, nut, bolt, and bracket. Make sure all components are tight and clear of the suspension and steering system.

A safety inspection includes checking every nut, bolt, and washer that was installed during the upgrade. If something looks or feels wrong, don't be afraid to take the bracket or caliper apart and reassemble it correctly.

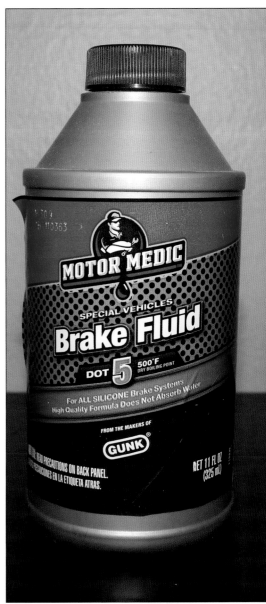

Wilwood Engineering and the other aftermarket brake manufacturers routinely release new products and work on new procedures for testing and installing their products. Even professional installers encourage following the instructions and procedures from these manufacturers exactly as written.

Brake fluids come in two basic types: glycol- or silicone-based fluids. The glycol-based brake fluids are labeled under the DOT3, DOT4, Super DOT4 and DOT5.1 standards. DOT5 stands alone as a silicon-based brake fluid and is not compatible with the other brake fluids. The DOT5 brake fluid is not recommended in road vehicles with anti-lock braking systems (ABS). Silicone brake fluids are not as corrosive as glycol-based brake fluids and do not absorb water like others do, but they do not provide the lubrication properties necessary for ABS pumps.

Bleeding the Brakes

After the brake system is installed, brake fluid is required to actuate the brake pads and stop the car. Many aftermarket brake companies offer their own branded brake fluids. For example, Wilwood has its Hi-Temp 570 grade fluid. The company also offers EXP 600 Plus Racing Brake Fluid for severe braking or sustained high-heat operation.

Most brake kit instructions explain that a Glycol-ether brake fluid (DOT3, DOT4, and DOT5.1) maintains a constant viscosity under a wide range of temperatures, including extreme hot and cold. These DOT-rated fluids will work in most brake systems with no problem.

Fill the reservoir with brake fluid and flush the system to prevent contamination of the new parts. Baer Brakes reminds its users to pour the brake fluid into the reservoir slowly to prevent aerating the fluid. Most aftermarket brake companies warn against using DOT5 silicone brake fluid in high-performance and racing applications.

Wilwood's EXP 600 Plus Racing Brake Fluid is manufactured to resist temperatures generated in harsh racing applications. This fluid is designed to be changed more often than a street-type brake fluid. Using the correct brake fluid for each application is as critical as using the correct brake pads. (Photo Courtesy of Wilwood Engineering Inc.)

An assistant is needed to help bleed the brakes. It will help significantly to explain the procedure to the assistant so he or she will understand the goal of the process. If a new master cylinder has been installed, it is important to bench bleed the master cylinder to purge any air bubbles inside the passages in the master cylinder before installation. Follow the directions with the new master cylinder for bench bleeding.

To bleed the rest of the brake system correctly, start the bleeding process with the caliper farthest away from the master cylinder. If the master cylinder is located in the stock position, start the bleeding process with the right rear caliper. If the caliper has two bleed screws, begin with the outside bleed screw first.

Attach a clear plastic bleed line to the bleeder screw at the caliper, have your assistant slowly press down on the brake pedal while you open the bleed screw. Your assistant should continue to push slowly on the brake pedal, repeating the process until fluid comes out of the bleeder. Close the bleed screw while your assistant is holding the brake pedal down toward the floor.

Have your assistant release the brake pedal, then slowly push the pedal, holding it down while you open the bleeder screw to release any additional air bubbles, then tighten the bleeder screw. Continue this process until no more air bubbles come out of the bleeder.

Before moving to the next caliper, use a rubber mallet and tap the caliper to release any air bubbles in the passages inside the caliper. Bleed the caliper one last time to check for any air bubbles freed by the mallet strike. Check and refill the master cylinder reservoir, then move to the inside bleeder screw if equipped. If not, move to the left rear caliper and perform the entire operation again.

Once you have completed the bleeding process for the left rear, move to the right front caliper and perform the same bleeding process as you did in the rear. The final caliper will be the left front. Have your assistant test the brake pedal. It should be firm, not spongy, and stop at least 1 inch from the floor under heavy load.

If the brake pedal feels spongy, the entire brake system should be bled again. If the brake pedal feels

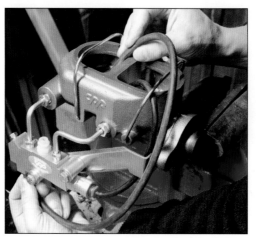

Getting rid of air bubbles in the brake system helps make a firm pedal. Air bubbles in the system causes a spongy pedal feel because air bubbles compress, and brake fluid does not. Bench bleeding the master cylinder is critical to eliminating the brake system of any air bubbles and is a straightforward job. The master cylinder should be bled before it is installed on the vehicle and before the rest of the system is bled.

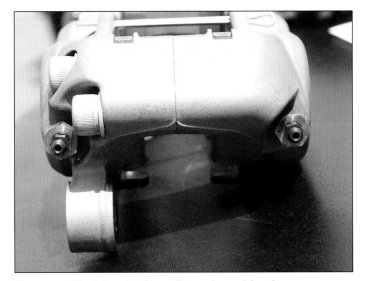

Some multi-piston brake calipers have bleed screws on the inside and outside of the caliper. These calipers have internal passages that the fluid flows through. Others may have an external transfer line that the fluid passes from one side of the caliper to the other. If the caliper has two bleed screws, begin bleeding the outside bleed screw first. If the caliper has two bleed screws on the same side but one on top and one on bottom, this is for mounting on either side of the vehicle. Only use the top bleed screw to bleed the caliper.

Residual valves and proportioning valves are an important part of your brake system's operation. This combination valve attached inline from the master cylinder has a warning light that detects a loss of pressure, a proportioning valve that regulates the pressure front and rear, a metering valve that applies pressure to the rear brakes first, and a residual check valve that prevents flow-back.

firm initially and then sinks to the floor, there is either a leak or a bleeder screw was not tightened securely. Check for leaks, fix the problem, and bleed the system again.

According to the engineers at Wilwood, if the brake pedal goes to the floor and continued bleeding of the system does not correct the problem, a master cylinder with increased capacity (a larger bore diameter) will be required. Of course, Wilwood (and other aftermarket manufacturers) offer various lightweight master cylinders with larger fluid displacement capacities.

Wilwood's Michael Hamrick also reminded us that master cylinder mounting location is critical when bleeding the system. Many hot rods and slammed vehicles mount the master cylinders in different locations.

"If the master cylinder is mounted lower than the disc brake calipers, some fluid flow-back to the master cylinder reservoir may occur, creating a vacuum effect that retracts the caliper pistons into the housing," said Hamrick. "This will cause the pedal to go to the floor on the first stroke until it has 'pumped up' and moved all the pistons out against the pad again."

Wilwood and other companies offer an in-line residual pressure valve that will stop this fluid flow-back and keep the pedal pressure firm when it is installed near the master cylinder.

The brake system's master cylinder location is normally on the firewall, but some systems use a different pedal box with the master cylinder located much lower. The location of the master cylinder is critical when bleeding the brake system. Brake fluid will often drain back to the master cylinder is if is mounted lower than the other brake components.

Routine After-Assembly Test

After the last lug nut has been installed and the car is ready to be lowered, resist the urge to jump in and drive around the block to see how well the new brake system operates. Under no circumstances should anyone drive on untested brakes on public roads with other traffic. This puts yourself and others in danger. After installation, a minimal test procedure should be undertaken before getting on a busy street with other vehicles.

Brake pressure speaks volumes. One of the easiest ways to check for problems is to make sure the pedal pressure is firm. Step on the brake pedal and hold steady pressure on the pedal for several minutes. The pedal should stay in the same position without lowering to the floor. If the pedal should lose position and sink toward the floor, the system probably has a leak somewhere and the entire system should be checked for fluid leaks.

Obviously, the car should not be driven if the pedal does not hold its position or drops to the floor during the test. This is a great time to have an assistant check the rear brake lights, and don't forget any brake warning lights on the dash. Test the parking brake (if equipped) to make sure it works properly.

If the static pressure test is good, a very low-speed test can be started. Always test the vehicle in a safe place where there is no danger to other people, vehicles, or yourself. An empty parking lot or a deserted road works well. Always wear seat belts and make use of all safety equipment.

By low speed, we mean no faster than a person can comfortably walk. Somewhere between 2 and 5 mph should be adequate. At that speed, apply the brakes hard several times. At

Always choose a location that is out of the way or an empty parking lot to do any testing or practice. Remember to check your brakes in a straight line and on left and right turns. Pay attention to any judder, pulling, or pressure drop.

the same time, the driver should turn the steering wheel from lock-to-lock, full left to full right while hitting the brakes very firmly several times. Park the car and lift it off the ground.

Remove the wheels and do a visual check to verify that no parts are touching, rubbing, or leaking. Take your time and carefully examine the brake system for any interference with wheels, suspension, or steering components. If it all checks out, reinstall the wheels and do a higher-speed test.

Increase the speed to 15 to 20 mph and perform another round of testing by hard braking while turning the steering wheel from full left to full right. Ensure that the brake pedal pressure feels normal and maintains position.

After several rounds of hard braking, pull the car back into the garage

Perform a visual inspection of the system after the initial low-speed testing. Check for any indication of component interference, rubbing, or other damage. Check for any leakage of brake fluid on the lines or where the lines connect. Any problems should be fixed before continuing.

When inspecting the brake system, it is easiest to pull the wheel and tire off the vehicle. This will give you an unobstructed view of the entire system and the opportunity to spot small leaks that you may miss with the wheel in place.

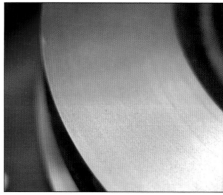

The brake rotor surface should be pristine and free of any film or materials before the bedding-in process can begin. The rotors and pads must be broken in together for the best long-term and trouble-free results. The bedding-in process is a matter of exposing the rotors and pads to a series of heat cycles.

and check for leaks and interference again. If everything checks out, reinstall the wheels and lower the vehicle to the ground.

Finally, conduct a straight-line stopping test. Choose a level, dry, hard surface that is free from any loose material, such as gravel, ice, or snow. An empty parking lot works well for this test. Drive in a straight line at 20 mph and firmly apply the brakes without skidding. The car should stop in a straight line, smoothly, in under 25 feet. Using a parking lot has advantages in conducting this test due to the markings on the pavement. These markings will help assess if your car is stopping in a straight line or pulling in one direction. The parking stalls will help with measuring stopping distance as well. If everything checks out well, continue on to the break-in procedure.

Breaking in the Brake Pads and Rotors

Like many components, brake pads and rotors need to be broken in for these parts to work together well and for a long time. This process is called bedding in. All brake pads and rotors must be bedded in together to maximize brake performance.

Simply stated, the bedding-in process is one of gradually building up heat in the pads and rotors. This process lays down a thin layer of brake pad material, a film, on the surface of the rotor. Laying down this thin film helps minimize brake judder.

Brake judder is the vibration when the brakes are applied. This vibration can be so minute that is it not noticeable, or it can be a very distinguishable shudder that is felt through the brake pedal or steering wheel. Following the manufacturer's bed-in procedures will ensure that a smooth, even layer of transfer film on the rotor will exist to combat the judder.

To bed-in new brake pads properly, the brake rotors should be new or resurfaced. The old transfer film from the previous pads need to be removed so the compound from the new brake pads provides the material for the transfer film. Before resurfacing rotors, check for excessive

Brake rotors that are not bedded in properly, or overheated, can cause a judder when the brakes are applied. A judder can be slight enough to be unnoticeable or severe enough to be a distraction. A judder generated in the front brakes can often be felt in the steering wheel.

run-out with a dial indicator gauge before sending it out to be resurfaced.

It is strongly encouraged to use the bed-in procedure from the manufacturer of the brake pads and rotor that you are using. This keeps you in warranty compliance and will ensure a long, trouble-free life of the brake components. Below is a generic procedure for bedding in brake pads and rotors for all pad compounds. This is the bare minimum and should be followed if no procedure is included in the kit you have purchased.

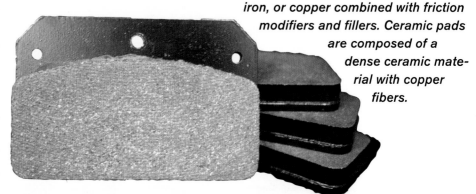

The single most improved area in the brake systems over the past 50 years has been in the brake pad material. Organic brake pads are composed of fibers such as glass, fiber, rubber, carbon, and Kevlar mixed with binding resins to hold them together. Semimetallic pads contain a percentage of steel, iron, or copper combined with friction modifiers and fillers. Ceramic pads are composed of a dense ceramic material with copper fibers.

Bedding-In Steps

After the brake system has been installed and tested as discussed above, the bedding-in procedure can be initiated. The procedure should be undertaken on a closed track or safe roadway where speeds of 65 mph can be legally obtained, followed by a rapid deceleration without posing a safety risk.

Start with a short series of very light decelerations to bring the heat up in the brake pads and rotors. Most professionals recommend to apply the brakes for 3 to 5 seconds and release the pedal for 6 to 10 seconds before applying the brakes again. Some professionals use a vocal count of 5 on the brakes with a count of 10 off for a cycle to allow the heat to sink into the pads and rotor.

After several cycles of light stops, the brakes should begin to warm sufficiently to continue with a series of medium to firm braking cycles to continue raising the heat level in the brakes.

The bedding-in cycle can then continue with 8 to 10 hard decelerations from highway speeds of 55 to 65 mph down to 25 mph. Use the

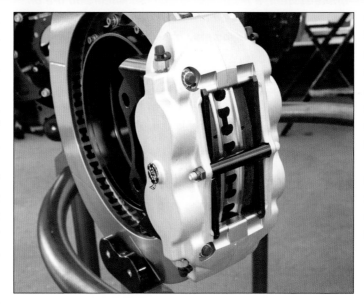

Cooling vanes vary in size and shape depending on the manufacturer and the application the rotors are designed for. These cooling vanes are often the best method of controlling brake fade.

same amount of time to release the braking and allow the heat-sinking process to continue between cycles. The pads should have a positive and consistent feel during braking. If any brake fade is noticed during the bed-in cycles, begin the cool-down process immediately.

From here you can drive at a moderate speed, using the brakes minimally, until most of the heat has dissipated from the brakes. Park the vehicle and allow the brakes to cool

down to ambient air temperature. For street vehicles, the bedding-in process is complete.

For track-only vehicles with brake cooling ducts, turning off the cooling fans or blocking the ducts will allow the pads and rotors to heat up quicker and speed up the bedding-in process. For race vehicles, always get heat into the brakes prior to each event. This will help to ensure best consistency, performance, and durability from your brakes.

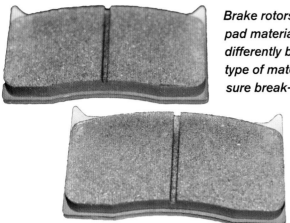

Brake rotors and brake pad materials break in differently based on the type of material. Make sure break-in procedures that come with your kit are followed if they are provided.

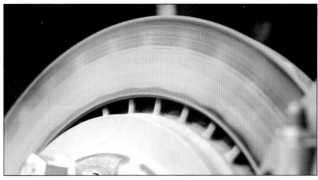

Uneven wear and overheating are signs of an abused brake system. This vehicle with stock brakes is a prime candidate for a brake system upgrade.

Post Bedding-In Inspection

After the bedding-in procedure has been accomplished, the rotors should have a burnished finish across the rotor face. Look for any splotching that would signify that the brakes were brought up to temperature too quickly in the bedding-in process.

If the brakes begin to exhibit noticeable brake judder, the rotors may need to be resurfaced and the bedding-in process accomplished again to restore a transfer film to the uniform surface of the rotor.

The Last Word

Now that you upgraded to a new disc brake system on your classic muscle car, you've probably realized how transformed the ride really feels. The amount of control that a nice set of brakes brings to these classics is truly impressive.

No longer do you need to plan to stop or worry about cars pulling out in front of you on crowded highways. Your pride and joy will stop as well as anything on the road and give you confidence in the car's abilities. Now, enjoy and share the ride with others. We call that money and time well spent!

A used brake rotor should be resurfaced when new brake pads are installed. The old material from the previous pads needs to be removed so the compound from the new brake pads can provide the transfer film on the new surface. Make sure to check runout before sending the rotors out to be resurfaced.

Nothing is more satisfying than selecting a brake upgrade, doing the work yourself, and taking your machine out to the local track and measuring the difference. Brakes are the one area where slowing down result in faster lap times. A well-planned and executed brake upgrade is not only safer, it can be quicker.

SOURCE GUIDE

AFCO Racing
977 Hyrock Blvd.
Boonville, IN 47601
800-632-2320
afcodynapro.com/afco

Akebono
19-5, Nihonbashi Koami-cho,
    Chou-Ku
Tokyo 103-8534, Japan
81-3-3668-5171
akebonobrakes.com

Baer Brakes
2222 West Peoria Ave.
Phoenix, AZ 85029
602-233-1411
baer.com

Brembo
CURNO (Bergamo)
Via Brembo, 25 Italy
brembo.com/en

Classic Performance Products
    (CPP)
378 E. Orangethorpe Ave.
Placentia, CA 92870
714-522-2000
classicperform.com

DBA USA
3423 Southpark Pl., Ste. B
Grove City, OH 43123
800-747-2220
dbausa.com

EBC Brakes
6180 South Pearl St.
Las Vegas, NV 89120
702-826-2400
ebcbrakes.com

Master Power Brakes
110 Crosslake Park Dr.
Mooresville, NC 28117
800-472-4181
mpbrakes.com

Performance Friction Brakes
    (PFC Brakes)
83 Carbon Metallic Highway
Clover, SC 29710
800-521-8874
pfcbrakes.com

Power Stop
6112 W. 73rd St.
Bedford Park, IL 60638
888-863-4415
powerstop.com

Speedway Motors
340 Victory Lane
Lincoln, NE 68528
800-979-0122
speedwaymotors.com

SSBC Performance Brake
    Systems
11470 Main Rd.
Clarence, NY 14031
800-448-7722
ssbrakes.com

TBM Brakes
838 Calle Plano
Camarillo, CA 93012
805-987-7867
tbmbrakes.com

Wagner Brakes
800-325-8886
wagnerbrake.com

Wilwood Engineering Inc.
4700 Calle Bolero
Camarillo, CA 93012
805-388-1188
wilwood.com